SIMPLY
SUGAR FREE

SIMPLY
SUGAR FREE

DELICIOUS SUGAR-FREE RECIPES FOR HEALTHIER EATING EVERY DAY

SUSANNA BOOTH

hamlyn

Contents

Introduction

You may wonder why a book of no added sugar recipes is full of sweet foods. Obviously, the way to avoid most sugar is simply never to eat anything sweet. However, eating is so much more than mere refuelling. It is bound up with social convention, our emotions and the habits we have developed over time.

I love sweet things. Whether it's a little something to finish off a meal, a mid-morning snack or a full-on overblown dessert for special occasions, I feel life would be incredibly diminished if I could eat only savoury foods for the rest of it. But I also know that too much sweet food is bad for my health – dental and otherwise. Unless we are clawing our way across Antarctica in a blizzard, our daily nutritional needs for sugar are small.

The key is balance: some sweetness, but not too much; a good variety of foods; plenty of fibre; lots of vitamins; small portions. We all know it, but it's often easier said than done.

It is in this spirit that I have developed this book. Whatever your reasons for wanting to cut back on sugar, this collection of recipes can help. They combine the natural sweetness of fruits and vegetables with whole grains, nuts and seeds to offer healthier alternatives to many of our favourite sugary dishes and treats.

Some of the cakes, ice creams and desserts may be less sweet than those you've grown used to because it has become the norm for foods to contain high levels of sugar. But I believe that if you want to move away from a reliance on sugar, an important step is to become accustomed to things being a little less sweet. You'll find that quite quickly you won't notice a difference and may even experience a heightened sense of taste.

You'll soon see how easy and rewarding it is to go sugar free – no junk, just a sweeter way to live.

Susanna Booth

The Role of Sugar in the Diet

WHAT IS SUGAR?

Table sugar, granulated sugar, demerara sugar, muscovado sugar, caster sugar… these familiar forms of sugar are all a substance known scientifically as sucrose. Sucrose is extracted from the juice of sugar cane or sugar beet and then processed and purified. The degree of refining affects the colour and size of the crystals, but they are basically all the same product. Molasses and black treacle are by-products of sugar processing that still contain a high level of sucrose. All sugars have four calories per gram.

Sugar is a naturally derived product – the problem with it is that any vitamins, minerals or fibre that were present in the original plant have been removed. This is why it is thought of as 'empty calories' – it offers us energy, but nothing else that the body can use. This may be useful occasionally, but most of the time it's just not necessary, and can even be harmful.

Chemically speaking, 'sugar' is a word used to describe a group of related molecules. They are made up of carbon, hydrogen and oxygen atoms, which is why they are also part of a larger group called carbohydrates. Sucrose is in fact made up of two simpler sugars – fructose and glucose – joined together, a bit like when you link two paperclips. Combinations of glucose or fructose molecules create many common carbohydrates, including fructo-oligosaccharides, maltose, maltodextrin, starch and cellulose (fibre).

Glucose (also known as dextrose)

Glucose is found in a variety of foods: as well as fruit, it also occurs in low levels in grains, beans and vegetables. It is also added to food; it's a major component of glucose syrup.

Our cells rely on glucose to work – it's literally the fuel we need to survive. One of the main goals of our digestive system is to ensure glucose gets into our blood in order to be carried around the body to the cells.

Ideally, our bodies would like a steady trickle of glucose rather than a massive dose all at once. The extent to which foods raise the level of glucose in our bloodstream after eating gives us the 'Glycaemic Index' rating, more commonly known as GI. Pure glucose is rated 100, with other foods ranked in descending order. Unless we have been exercising strenuously, it's best to opt for foods with GI ratings of 65 and below, or combine a high-GI food (such as white bread with a GI of 70) with foods that either don't contain sugars or very low amounts (for example, foods that aren't carbohydrates, like eggs, meat, green vegetables, cheese or cream).

Too much glucose can cause health problems, as highlighted on page 8.

Fructose (also known as laevulose)

Fructose is sometimes called 'fruit sugar' because it is found in nearly all fruits. It tastes much sweeter than sucrose. After eating, it's transported to the liver, where much of it is converted to glucose. This means that its GI rating is low because the process is fairly slow.

Our ancestors would probably never have consumed more fructose in a day than that which was in the fruit/honey they ate, but these days it's possible to consume considerably more. This has been linked to a variety of health problems – see page 8 for more on this.

Problems caused by sugar

When glucose is produced during digestion, it enters the bloodstream and a hormone called insulin is released. Insulin helps certain cells store some of the glucose in a different form, called glycogen. The result is that the blood glucose levels fall to normal. If the levels drop below normal, glycogen is turned back into glucose. When the brain detects higher glucose levels, it stops hunger signals, which is why a steady intake of glucose (such as that created when complex carbohydrates are digested) helps to keep you feeling full for longer.

On a day-to-day level, eating too much sugary food in one go will result in a sudden large increase in blood glucose levels, only for them to drop very quickly. This could contribute to mood swings and tiredness, and can also make you feel very hungry again relatively quickly, which could lead to excess calorie consumption.

Excessive glucose

As described above, insulin is used to control the levels of glucose in the blood, with the excess being stored as glycogen. However, the body can only store a certain amount of glucose in this way, and any beyond that limit is converted to fat. A large excess can therefore lead to obesity.

Diabetes is the name given to a disease where insulin is either not produced at all, not produced in high enough concentrations or is faulty. This means that the level of glucose in the blood stays high. Left untreated, it can cause severe health complications.

Excessive fructose

Fructose, as mentioned before, is converted into glucose in the liver. However, the body is not able to absorb large amounts, so some of it is left over to be devoured by our gut bacteria instead. The bacteria release gas, which can lead to bloating and diarrhoea. Some people have difficulty absorbing even small amounts of fructose, a condition known as fructose malabsorption.

Processing high levels of fructose also produces uric acid, which can result in gout, and has been linked to a higher risk of obesity and high blood pressure.

Sugar and teeth

Inside our mouths lives a colony of bacteria. These bacteria like sticking themselves to our teeth using a sort of starchy glue, which is also their food – we call this plaque. The bacteria make this glue by digesting carbohydrates found in our mouths, especially sugars like glucose, fructose, sucrose and maltose. As they digest the sugar, an acid is produced. It is this acid that damages our tooth enamel and leads to decay.

These bacteria have always lived with us, but examination of the skulls of our ancestors from a thousand or so years ago often shows little tooth decay despite the lack of toothbrushes, toothpaste etc. It seems that a combination of tough, fibrous breads, vegetables and meat (lots of chewing) and limited sweet foods helped to keep the levels of plaque in check. In the UK, the widespread increase in tooth decay dates only from about 1600 onwards – the time when large amounts of refined sugar became freely available.

Modern dental advice suggests brushing before breakfast, eating sweet foods only as part of a meal, avoiding 'grazing' on sweet/starchy foods, drinking plenty of water (which rinses away sugars and acids) and brushing again before bed. Eating hard cheese or peanuts after a meal will help to make the mouth less acidic as well.

SUGAR ALTERNATIVES

There is no magic alternative to sugar – all have pros and cons. Some are naturally derived, such as sugar alcohols (maltitol, xylitol and others) and stevia, though humans have never before been able to eat them to excess, while others are man-made, as in the artificial sweeteners, the long-term effects of which are still not fully known. Other options like honey, maple syrup or fruit and vegetables still contain sucrose, glucose and fructose, so in that respect they are not much different to table sugar.

Of all of them, using whole fruit and vegetables as sweeteners seems to me the most preferable because, not only are they 'real foods', but there are also many added benefits. This is why I have based most of the recipes in this book around fruit and vegetables. Fruit and vegetables, whether fresh or dried, almost all contain some level of sugar, be it sucrose, glucose, fructose or all three. Some fruits – and especially dried fruits like dates or raisins – can be considered high-sugar foods and therefore you need to watch how much you eat. However, they offer many added benefits, such as fibre and an assortment of vitamins and minerals. Large amounts of fibre help you to feel full, which should support portion control.

Where a little extra sweetness is required, I have used small quantities of stevia because it is naturally derived and does not cause tooth decay, but feel free to substitute it with a different sweetener if you prefer.

What is stevia?

Stevia rebaudiana is a plant with white flowers found in Brazil and Paraguay. Its leaves contain a cocktail of related chemicals called steviol glycosides (including steviosides and rebaudiosides), which have a sweetness over 200 times stronger than sucrose. It also has a slightly bitter aftertaste, which

can be unpleasant. Stevia extracts are poorly metabolized, passing through the stomach and small intestine intact. Bacteria in the large intestine then break the molecules down.

The stevia you can buy usually involves a refined extract of the leaf, blended with another sugar substitute to bulk it out and improve the flavour. Though sweetening agents in stevia leaves have no GI, no calories and don't cause tooth decay, the bulking product may do, so check the label carefully.

Stevia extracts have been in use as a sweetener in Japan and other Asian countries for decades. In the European Union, stevia-based sweeteners were approved in 2011. Currently, the Food and Drug Administration (FDA) in the USA has not approved the whole leaf or crude extracts for use in food – only sweeteners using rebaudioside A have been accepted as GRAS (Generally Recognized As Safe). For more information, see www.fda.gov. Also, see page 187 for more about my use of stevia.

Simple Steps to Sugar-free Eating

LIVING WITHOUT SUGAR

Despite the popularity of 'paleo' diets that avoid grains, these kinds of complex carbohydrates have been the staple food of humans for thousands of years. For instance, the Romans, Ancient Greeks and Ancient Egyptians all ate wheat-based bread every day and the Ancient Chinese ate rice, while early South American peoples such as the Olmec ate maize. Whole grains are a great energy source and they also make us feel full.

What wasn't eaten in bulk throughout the year in ancient times was masses of sugary foods made of simple carbohydrates – be it cakes and biscuits or even honey or fruit. In excess, such foods are bad news for our bodies and our teeth. Indeed, some experts believe that high-sugar diets are the biggest health problem facing mankind today.

The World Heath Organization's current guidelines recommend no more than 50g (2oz/ 10 teaspoons) of added sugar (including that from honey, maple syrup, juice and fruit concentrates but not whole fruit and vegetables) per adult per day – you could reach this amount after just a bowl of cereal and a glass of orange juice. The WHO suggests that lowering that figure to a mere 25g (1oz/5 teaspoons) would be even more beneficial. It makes sense to choose your sweet foods carefully.

TOP TIPS FOR MINIMIZING SUGAR INTAKE

- **Avoid sweet drinks.** A can of full sugar cola contains 30–40g (around 6–8 teaspoons) of sugar, so this is a really easy place to start cutting back. Incredibly, a 300ml (½ pint) glass of fruit juice can often contain similar amounts – or even more! This is because it will be the juice of many fruits. Instead of drinking apple juice, for instance, eat an apple. It will taste just as sweet, but your total sugar consumption will be much lower and you'll have the benefit of the fibre as well.
- **Avoid sweetened sauces or dressings.** Salad cream, ketchup, sweet chilli sauce, pickle and even mustard can all contain sugar – these 'hidden' sugars can soon add up. Try vinaigrette or real mayonnaise as an alternative.
- **Be careful about breakfast choices.** Many cereals contain high levels of sugar. Instead opt for foods like porridge, eggs, natural yogurt or wholemeal bread with cheese.
- **Minimize alcohol consumption.** Alcohol is created when yeasts break down sugar. If that process isn't completed, sugar can remain, as in the case of sweet white wines, cider or beer. Spirits are a better choice, sugar-wise; use an unsweetened mixer like soda water.
- **Go raw and fresh where you can.** Many fruits taste sweeter raw than cooked, and food at room temperature will taste sweeter than the same food when frozen.
- **Sprinkle with powdered sweetener.** If you like adding sweetener to fruit or cereal, for example, a light dusting of a powdered product can often be just as effective taste-wise as a heavy sprinkling of granulated sugar or a drizzling of syrup.

COOKING WITHOUT SUGAR

As well as acting as a sweetener, sugar also plays a role in the texture of foods. For instance, it is sugar's ability to melt into a hard glass-like caramel that helps give the strength to a finished meringue or the 'snap' in certain kinds of biscuit. The fudgy texture of sugar heated with butter is what makes chewy cookies or brownies so moreish. And the presence of sugar is also an integral part of smooth ice creams and sorbets because it acts like antifreeze, preventing the growth of large ice crystals.

This means that successful cooking without sugar is not always just a matter of leaving it out or replacing it with another kind of sweetener because many of the alternatives don't behave in the same way. Careful thought is often required in order to achieve good results. I've tried to create healthy versions of favourite recipes – using whole foods where possible – that emulate the textures normally associated with those dishes. For instance, I use butternut squash to make my brownies chewy (see page 130), and for my squidgy cookies I use banana (see page 33). I've even managed to create silky ice creams with the help of agar powder, whose large molecular structure helps keep ice crystals to a minimum (see page 186).

TOP TIPS FOR CREATING SUGAR-FREE RECIPES

- **Mix stevia powder with liquid before use.** Stevia is so super-sweet that its granules can taste unpleasant, while its bitter flavours can be noticeable when used in large amounts. I've found I get the best results when I dissolve it in liquid before adding it to my recipe. Add it gradually – it's surprising how little you need.
- **Stick to 'nuggets' of sweetness.** Sometimes this is all that's necessary to make something tasty. If your cake has small pieces of sweet foods, such as raisins, chopped apricots and pieces of fruit, you can reduce the sweetness of the cake mixture without really noticing.
- **Try to exploit naturally sweet foods.** Rice milk, evaporated milk, cashew nuts, fresh fruit, dried fruit and vegetables like carrots are among the foods that are naturally sweet. If you add them to recipes you can cut back on added sweeteners.
- **Opt for the freshest, best-quality apple juice or orange juice**. Cloudy apple juices and the type of orange juice that still has bits both have more micronutrients than the juices that have been filtered and concentrated.
- **Be creative with toppings.** One of the drawbacks of going sugar free is that most cake toppings (be it icing sugar, frosting or sugar sprinkles) involve sugar in some form. Try decorating cakes with whipped cream, cream cheese, whole nuts or fresh or dried fruit instead. Wafer shapes, cocoa powder, edible glitter and edible flowers are great for achieving that final wow factor.
- **Use whole foods where possible.** This can include seeds, whole nuts, whole grains, whole fruit and vegetables (try to keep the skin on if you can). You might only include a small amount, but that doesn't matter – some is always better than none.
- **Eat smart.** Using sugar alternatives is not a licence to eat large amounts of sweet foods. Keeping portion sizes small and infrequent means that you can still enjoy cakes and desserts, but overall sugar consumption will be lower.

Recipe Finder

MUFFINS, COOKIES & CUPCAKES

	Page	Dairy-free	Gluten-free	Contains no eggs	Contains no nuts	Vegetarian	Vegan
Double Chocolate Muffins	17	○	○	○	●	●	○
Cherry & Almond Muffins	18	●	○	○	○	●	○
Seeded Breakfast Muffins	20	●	○	○	○	●	○
Sage Muffins with Sour Cream & Bacon	21	○	○	○	●	○	○
Roquefort & Pear Muffins	22	○	○	○	○	●	○
Hazelnut Cappuccino Cupcakes	25	○	○	○	○	●	○
Lemon Coconut Cupcakes	27	○	○	○	●	●	○
Cinnamon Thins	28	○	○	●	●	●	○
Salted Lime Sandwich Biscuits	30	○	○	●	●	●	○
Oatmeal Raisin Cookies	32	●	○	●	○	●	○
Date & Walnut Cookies	33	○	○	●	○	●	○
Almond & Fig Cookies	34	○	○	○	○	●	○
Chocolate Hazelnut Palmiers	37	○	○	●	○	●	○
Strawberry Scones	38	○	○	○	●	●	○

CAKES & GATEAUX

	Page	Dairy-free	Gluten-free	Contains no eggs	Contains no nuts	Vegetarian	Vegan
Chocolate Tea Cake	43	○	○	○	●	●	○
Apricot & Lemon Cake	44	●	●	○	○	●	○
Sticky Date & Apple Cake	46	○	○	○	●	●	○
Fruit Cake	47	○	○	○	○	●	○
Nectarine Upside Down Cake	48	○	○	○	●	●	○
Spicy Ginger Cake with Apricot Topping	50	○	○	○	○	●	○
Carrot Cake	51	○	○	○	○	●	○
Gateau Marcel with Cherries & Blueberries	53	●	○	○	●	●	○
Chestnut Tiramisu Cake	54	○	●	○	○	●	○
Pear Kuchen	55	○	○	○	○	●	○
Red Velvet Cake	56	○	○	●	●	●	○
Portuguese Custard Tarts	58	○	○	●	●	●	○
Raspberry Tarts	61	○	○	○	●	●	○

DESSERTS

	Page	Dairy-free	Gluten-free	Contains no eggs	Contains no nuts	Vegetarian	Vegan
Clementine & Pomegranate Jelly	65	●	●	●	●	●	○
Jewelled Chocolate Tart	66	○	○	○	○	●	○
Mandarin Cheesecake	68	○	○	○	●	●	○
Creamy Almond Rice with Balsamic Figs	69	○	●	●	○	●	○
Poached Pears with Mascarpone	70	○	●	●	●	●	○
Chocolate Mousse	72	○	●	○	●	●	○
Apple Tortilla	73	○	○	○	●	●	○
Tropical Roulade	75	○	●	○	●	●	○
Plum Tarts	76	○	○	●	●	●	○
Banana & Orange Filo Parcels	77	○	○	●	●	●	○
Pineapple Meringue	78	○	●	○	●	●	○
Raspberry & Mint Sundae	80	○	●	●	●	●	○
Peach Fruit Fool	81	○	●	●	●	●	○
Fresh Fig Panna Cotta	82	○	●	●	●	●	○
Fragrant Fruit Salad	84	●	●	●	●	●	●

ICE CREAMS

	Page	Dairy-free	Gluten-free	Contains no eggs	Contains no nuts	Vegetarian	Vegan
Chocolate Chip Ice Cream	89	○	●	○	●	●	○
Vanilla Ice Cream	89	○	●	○	●	●	○
Banana & Salted Peanut Ice Cream	90	○	●	●	○	●	○
Papaya & Lime Ice Cream	91	○	●	●	●	●	○
Strawberry Parfait	92	○	●	○	●	●	○
Pistachio Kulfi	94	○	●	●	○	●	○
Lychee Frozen Yogurt	95	○	●	●	●	●	○
Ginger Granita	96	●	●	●	●	●	●
Piña Colada Ice	98	●	●	●	●	●	○
Orange & Star Anise Sorbet	99	●	●	●	●	●	○
Campari & Watermelon Lollies	101	●	●	●	●	●	●

EVERYDAY SNACKS

	Page	Dairy-free	Gluten-free	Contains no eggs	Contains no nuts	Vegetarian	Vegan
Cream Cheese & Apple Twists	104			●	●	●	
Peanut Snack Bars	106	●		●		●	●
Chocolate & Rye Energy Bars	108			●		●	
Raw Gingerbread	109	●		●		●	●
Banana Bread	111				●	●	
Cardamom Waffles with Berries	112				●	●	
Swedish Cherry Buns	114				●	●	
Fruit Plait	117			●	●	●	
Apple Porridge	118			●	●	●	
Mango & Cranberry Muesli	119	●		●		●	●
Poppy Seed Grissini	120			●	●	●	
Smoked Cheese & Apple Scones	121				●	●	
Spiced Trail Mix	123	●	●	●		●	●
Pumpkin Pops	123	●		●	●	●	●

FOR CHILDREN

	Page	Dairy-free	Gluten-free	Contains no eggs	Contains no nuts	Vegetarian	Vegan
Cheesy Breadsticks	126			●	●	●	
Tomato & Herb Spirals	129			●	●	●	
Chocolate Brownies	130				●	●	
Magic Pancakes	133				●	●	
Apple Freezer Flapjacks	134			●		●	
Chocolate Refrigerator Cake	135			●		●	
Sticky Doughnut Buns	136				●	●	
Ginger Stars	138			●	●	●	
Crispy Cakes	139	●	●			●	
Apple & Blackberry Parcels	141			●		●	
Pineapple Fritters	142				●	●	
Stripy Snow Cones	145	●	●	●	●	●	●

TREATS & PARTY FOOD

	Page	Dairy-free	Gluten-free	Contains no eggs	Contains no nuts	Vegetarian	Vegan
Glittering Chocolate Truffles	148		●	●	●	●	
Apricot Hearts	151	●	●	●		●	
Mini Chocolate Eclairs	152				●	●	
Rocky Road	154			●		●	
Macadamia Chews	155	●	●	●		●	
Chocolate Fondue	157		●	●	● ●	●	
Baklava	159					●	
Mint Chocolate Crunch	160			●		●	
Cinnamon Toasts	161				●	●	
Toffee-flavoured Popcorn	162		●	●		●	
Sweet Chilli Bites	163		●	●	●	●	
Butter-fried Plantains with Smoky Dip	165		●	●	●	●	

SAUCES, SPREADS & OTHER BASICS

	Page	Dairy-free	Gluten-free	Contains no eggs	Contains no nuts	Vegetarian	Vegan
Velvet Hot Chocolate	168		●	●		●	
Low-carb Dessert Pastry	170				●	●	
Whipped Cake Frosting	171	●	●	●		●	
Vanilla Cream	172	●	●	●		●	
Orange Dessert Sauce	173	●	●	●		●	
Mango Coulis	174	●	●	●	●	●	●
Mixed Berry Compote	175	●	●	●	●	●	●
Orange & Apricot Curd	176		●			●	
Strawberry Jam	178	●	●	●	●	●	●
Chocolate Hazelnut Spread	179	●	●	●		●	
Quick Apple Pickle	180	●	●	●	●	●	●
Asian-style Dipping Sauce	181	●		●	●	●	●
Tomato Ketchup	182	●	●	●	●	●	●
Avocado Mayonnaise	184	●	●	●	●	●	●
Vinaigrette Dressing	185	●	●	●	●	●	●

Please note this is a guideline only; all ingredients
should be checked for suitability before use.

Muffins, Cupcakes & Cookies

Airy chocolate muffins oozing little nuggets of melted chocolate are one of the finest sights to emerge from an oven. Even better is the fact that muffins benefit from a laid-back approach, so this is seriously easy baking that anyone can master.

Double Chocolate Muffins

MAKES 12

225g (7½oz) plain flour
3 tablespoons cocoa powder
3 teaspoons baking powder
250ml (8fl oz) rice milk
125ml (4fl oz) sunflower oil
3 eggs, beaten
2 teaspoons unsweetened vanilla
   extract
2 teaspoons stevia powder
   (see page 187)
150g (5oz) no-added-sugar milk
   chocolate, chopped into chunks

Preheat the oven to 180°C/160°C fan/350°F/Gas Mark 4. Line a 12-cup muffin tin with paper muffin cases.

Mix the flour, cocoa powder and baking powder together in a bowl. Stir the rice milk, oil, eggs, vanilla extract and stevia powder together in a jug.

Pour the liquid mixture into the bowl and give a quick stir. It doesn't matter if there are still a few lumps – undermixing is better than stirring for too long, which can lead to a chewy, rather than airy, texture. Stir in the chocolate chunks.

You'll now have a sloppy brown mixture. Divide the muffin mixture evenly between the muffin cases.

Bake the muffins for 15–30 minutes until risen and springy to the touch, and an inserted skewer comes out clean. Leave them to cool on a wire rack before serving. These muffins are lovely warm, but even better the following day. They also freeze well.

Almonds are one of nature's superfoods and combining them with cherries is a sure-fire way to get a tasty result. Almond milk gives an extra nutrient hit and also makes these muffins a dairy-free treat.

Cherry & Almond Muffins

MAKES 12

150g (5oz) ground almonds
150g (5oz) plain flour
3 teaspoons baking powder
175ml (6fl oz) unsweetened almond milk
85ml (3¼fl oz) sunflower oil
3 eggs, beaten
2 tablespoons stevia powder (see page 187)
1½ teaspoons unsweetened almond extract
300g (10oz) fresh cherries, pitted and halved
2 tablespoons flaked almonds

Preheat the oven to 200°C/180°C fan/400°F/Gas Mark 6. Line a 12-cup muffin tin with paper muffin cases.

Mix the ground almonds, flour and baking powder together in a bowl. Stir the almond milk, oil, eggs, stevia powder and almond extract together in a jug.

Pour the liquid mixture into the dry ingredients and give everything a quick stir until combined. Stir in the cherry halves.

Divide the muffin mixture evenly between the muffin cases. Sprinkle a few of the flaked almonds on top of each one.

Bake the muffins for 15–20 minutes until risen and golden brown, and an inserted skewer comes out clean. Leave them to cool on a wire rack. Store the muffins in the refrigerator and eat within a couple of days.

Forget sugary cereals and try these awesome muffins for breakfast instead. Filling and nutritious, the combination of superfoods and protein will give your morning just the boost it needs. I like to make a batch and pop them in the freezer, defrosting them in the microwave as needed so that I always have some to hand.

Seeded Breakfast Muffins

MAKES 12

225g (7½oz) plain flour
150g (5oz) drained canned sweetcorn kernels
150g (5oz) soft pitted prunes
50g (2oz) sunflower seeds
50g (2oz) carrot, peeled and finely grated
250ml (8fl oz) unsweetened almond milk
125ml (4fl oz) sunflower oil
3 eggs
3 teaspoons unsweetened vanilla extract
3 teaspoons baking powder
1 teaspoon ground cinnamon
2 tablespoons pumpkin seeds

Preheat the oven to 180°C/160°C fan/350°F/Gas Mark 4. Line a 12-cup muffin tin with paper muffin cases.

Place all the ingredients except the pumpkin seeds in a food processor and blend for 10–15 seconds until everything is combined.

Pour the muffin mixture into the muffin cases, ensuring you have distributed it evenly. Scatter the pumpkin seeds on the top of each muffin.

Bake the muffins for 25 minutes until risen and golden brown, and an inserted skewer comes out clean. Leave them to cool in the tin. These are great either warm or cold, perhaps spread with a little butter. Store the muffins in the refrigerator and eat within a couple of days.

Don't knock a savoury muffin until you've tried one, and few are as mouth-watering as these, with their light sage flavour and crowning dollop of soured cream and bacon.

Sage Muffins with Sour Cream & Bacon

MAKES 8

1 teaspoon sunflower oil
4 unsmoked streaky bacon rashers, finely chopped
125ml (4fl oz) soured cream
50g (2oz) Cheddar cheese or other hard cheese
150g (5oz) plain flour
1 tablespoon finely chopped sage
2 teaspoons baking powder
85ml (3¼fl oz) sunflower oil
175ml (6fl oz) milk
2 eggs

Preheat the oven to 200°C/180°C fan/400°F/Gas Mark 6. Line 8 cups of a 12-cup muffin tin with paper muffin cases.

Heat the oil in a frying pan and fry the chopped bacon until crisp. Stir the bacon bits into the soured cream and set aside.

Roughly grate the cheese into a bowl. Stir in the flour, sage and baking powder.

Whisk the oil, milk and eggs together in a separate bowl. Pour the eggy liquid into the flour mixture and give a good, brisk stir until everything is combined. You'll now have a sloppy mixture.

Pour the muffin mixture evenly into the muffin cases. Top each one with about a tablespoonful of the soured cream and bacon, dolloped into the centre.

Bake the muffins for 15 minutes until risen and browned – the soured cream will have remained at the top of each muffin. Leave the muffins to cool on a wire rack before serving. These are best eaten on the day they are made.

Tip

A mezzaluna, consisting of a single or double curved blade with a handle at either end, makes chopping fresh herbs incredibly easy and quick.

Roquefort cheese might seem a strange addition to muffins, but it works really well without being overly cheesy. My two-year-old will happily eat these, yet there is no way he would ever eat Roquefort, walnuts or, to be honest, even pears by themselves. These are delicious hot or cold, but best enjoyed on the day they are made.

Roquefort & Pear Muffins

MAKES 12

4 small Williams pears, about 400g (13oz) total weight
75g (3oz) Roquefort cheese or other blue cheese, crumbled
3 eggs
175ml (6fl oz) sunflower oil
4 tablespoons milk
1½ teaspoons unsweetened vanilla extract
100g (3½oz) wholemeal plain flour
100g (3½oz) white plain flour
4 teaspoons baking powder
100g (3½oz) walnuts, chopped

Preheat the oven to 200°C/180°C fan/400°F/Gas Mark 6. Line a 12-cup muffin tin with paper muffin cases.

Remove the cores from the pears (leave the skin on). Chop one into small chunks about 1cm (½ inch) in size and set aside. Place the remaining pears in a blender with the cheese, eggs, oil, milk and vanilla extract and blend until smooth.

Transfer to a bowl and stir in both flours and the baking powder, then stir in the walnuts and reserved chopped pear.

Divide the muffin mixture evenly between the muffin cases and bake for 20 minutes until risen and browned. Serve straight away or leave to cool on a wire rack before serving.

I have a total weakness for hazelnut lattes, a habit that I try to keep to an absolute minimum for the sake of my teeth and general health! It was, however, the inspiration for these cupcakes – they provide the nutty–coffee flavours and frothy sweetness that I love, just without a load of sugar.

Hazelnut Cappuccino Cupcakes

MAKES 12

3 tablespoons stevia powder
   (see page 187)
2 tablespoons instant coffee
2 teaspoons balsamic vinegar
2 tablespoons boiling water
50g (2oz) wholemeal plain flour
50g (2oz) white plain flour
75g (3oz) unsalted butter,
   very soft, chopped
2 eggs, beaten
1 teaspoon bicarbonate of soda
40g (1½oz) whole hazelnuts,
   chopped

For the topping
250ml (8fl oz) whipping cream
1 teaspoon stevia powder
   (see page 187)
½ teaspoon unsweetened vanilla
   extract
cocoa powder, for dusting

Preheat the oven to 180°C/160°C fan/350°F/Gas Mark 4. Line a 12-cup muffin tin with paper muffin cases.

Stir the stevia powder, instant coffee, balsamic vinegar and measurement boiling water together in a jug until you have a thick, dark liquid – it doesn't matter if the stevia hasn't completely dissolved.

Place both flours, butter, eggs and bicarbonate of soda in a bowl. Add the coffee mixture and whisk everything together for a minute until fluffy and well combined. Fold in the nuts, then dollop a tablespoonful of the cupcake mixture into each muffin case.

Bake for 12–15 minutes until risen and browned, and an inserted skewer comes out clean. Transfer to a wire rack and leave to cool completely.

To make the topping, whip the cream with the stevia powder and vanilla extract until it forms firm peaks. Place in a piping bag fitted with a large star nozzle then pipe on to the cupcakes. Finish by sifting cocoa powder on to the top of each one. The finished cupcakes should be kept in the refrigerator until ready to serve and are best eaten the same day.

Variation

For a different slant on this recipe, smear a little of my Chocolate Hazelnut Spread (see page 179) on the top of each cupcake instead of the sweetened cream.

The delicate creamy sweetness of coconut is used to full effect as a topping for moist lemon sponge. Coconut milk varies: for best results, choose coconut milk with at least 18 per cent fat, and avoid brands with added sodium metabisulphite, as it can have an unpleasant taste.

Lemon Coconut Cupcakes

MAKES 12

1 x 400ml (14fl oz) can coconut
   milk, chilled
3 tablespoons stevia powder
   (see page 187)
150g (5oz) plain flour
2 teaspoons baking powder
85ml (3¼fl oz) sunflower oil
2 eggs, beaten
grated rind of 1 unwaxed lemon
   and 2 tablespoons juice

For the topping
20g (¾oz) desiccated coconut
1 teaspoon stevia powder
   (see page 187)
125ml (4fl oz) whipping cream

Preheat the oven to 180°C/160°C fan/350°F/Gas Mark 4. Line a 12-cup muffin tin with paper muffin cases.

Open the can of coconut milk, then scoop out the thick coconut 'cream' from the top of the can into a large bowl and set aside. Pour 125ml (4fl oz) of the remaining watery coconut milk into a separate large bowl. Stir in the stevia powder, then add the flour, baking powder, oil, eggs and lemon rind and juice. Give everything a quick and thorough whisk and then divide the mixture evenly between the muffin cases.

Bake the cupcakes for 20 minutes until risen and just browned, and an inserted skewer comes out clean. Leave on a wire rack to cool completely.

To make the topping, gently toast the desiccated coconut in a dry frying pan for 2 minutes, stirring occasionally, until golden. Leave to cool completely.

Add the stevia powder to the reserved coconut 'cream'. Using an electric whisk, whip until it forms soft peaks – this may take up to 4 minutes. Whip the whipping cream until it forms firm peaks, then fold into the coconut cream. Use a tablespoon to swirl a dollop on to each of the cupcakes and sprinkle the tops of them with the toasted desiccated coconut. These cakes will keep for a couple of days in the refrigerator.

Variation

For a completely dairy-free alternative, make the topping using only the thick coconut 'cream' scooped from the can. Stir in 1 teaspoon stevia powder and a pinch of xanthan gum, then whisk until it forms firm peaks. Spread onto the cupcakes and sprinkle with dessicated coconut.

These buttery, wafer-thin biscuits are part Swedish pepparkaka and part delicate tuile. Their light and airy crispness makes them perfect served alongside coffee or as an accompaniment to ice cream. The apple and cinnamon flavour is just heavenly too.

Cinnamon Thins

MAKES 18

1 egg white
4 tablespoons unsweetened apple purée
2 teaspoons stevia powder (see page 187)
1 teaspoon ground cinnamon
35g (1¼oz) plain flour
25g (1oz) unsalted butter, melted

Preheat the oven to 160°C/140°C fan/325°F/Gas Mark 3. Line a couple of baking sheets with silicone baking paper.

Whisk the egg white in a bowl until it forms a thick froth, then whisk in the apple purée, stevia powder and cinnamon.

Stir the flour and melted butter together in a small bowl. Fold into the egg white mix until you have a pale brown, thick mixture.

Dollop a heaped teaspoonful of the mixture on to one of the baking sheets. Use the back of a tablespoon to smooth it out evenly into a round about 7cm (3 inches) in diameter and 1–2mm (about ¹⁄₁₆ inch) thick – use a cookie cutter as a guide if you want them perfectly round, or cut a circle out of a piece of card to make a template. Repeat until you have filled the baking sheets.

Bake the thins for about 30 minutes until they have darkened and look dry – start checking them after 20 minutes. Transfer them to a wire rack. They will still be soft while they are hot, but once they have cooled they should be completely hard and crisp. They will keep for about a week, stored in an airtight container.

These luscious and very grown-up sandwich biscuits feature a frozen lime cheesecake filling encased within salted crackers. Try them as a modern twist on ice cream in a cone, or serve as a quick and easy party snack.

Salted Lime Sandwich Biscuits

MAKES 6

grated rind of ½ unwaxed lime
   and 1½ tablespoons juice
1 tablespoon white rum
1 tablespoon stevia powder
   (see page 187)
2 tablespoons cream cheese
125ml (4fl oz) double cream
12 salted wholemeal crackers

Stir together the lime rind and juice, rum and stevia powder in a cup until the stevia has dissolved. Stir in the cream cheese until smooth.

Whip the cream in a jug (see Tip) until it forms firm peaks. Stir in the lime mixture. Sandwich a tablespoonful of the resulting rather sloppy cream between 2 crackers and press down lightly (the cream shouldn't ooze out from between the crackers). Repeat for the remaining crackers.

Place all the sandwich biscuits on a tray or plate and then freeze them for 15 minutes until the filling has become firm. They are now ready to eat.

Tip

A quick way to whip cream without it spattering everywhere is to pour it into a jug and to use a stick blender. This can work too well, in that it becomes easy to overwhip the cream, so go easy.

With just four ingredients, these cookies are simplicity itself, but none the worse for that. What makes them so irresistible is the way the chewy raisins burst through the oats, which have a lovely, almost buttery, crunch. Serve with a glass of milk for a perfect mid-morning pick-me-up.

Oatmeal Raisin Cookies

MAKES 35

300g (10oz) jumbo rolled oats
160g (5½oz) raisins
85ml (3¼fl oz) sunflower oil,
    plus extra for oiling
175ml (6fl oz) boiling water
plain flour, for dusting

Preheat the oven to 150°C/130°C fan/300°F/Gas Mark 2. Lightly oil a couple of baking sheets with a little sunflower oil.

Place the oats and half the raisins in a food processor. Pulse until you have a mixture with the texture of breadcrumbs. Add the oil and measurement boiling water and continue to pulse until everything comes together as a soft dough. Stir in the remaining raisins, then let the dough sit and absorb the moisture for a couple of minutes.

Roll out the dough on a worktop well dusted with flour to a thickness of 5mm (¼ inch). Use a 6cm (2½-inch) round cookie cutter to cut out rounds, rerolling the trimmings as necessary, until you have used up all the dough. Place the dough rounds on the baking sheets.

Bake for 45 minutes until the cookies are golden brown, then switch the oven off and leave the cookies in the oven for a further 20 minutes until they have become completely hard. Leave to cool completely on a wire rack and store in an airtight tin. They will keep for up to a week.

Variation

You can make a gluten-free version of these cookies by using gluten-free oats and dusting your worktop with cornflour when rolling out.

These are proper doughy cookies, with a crunchy crust and chewy centre. However, unlike regular cookies, these are full of fibre and other goodness.

Date & Walnut Cookies

MAKES 12

1 banana, about 150g (5oz)
75g (3oz) pitted soft dried dates
50g (2oz) wholemeal plain flour
25g (1oz) unsalted butter, cut into chunks, plus extra for greasing
75g (3oz) walnuts, chopped
4 tablespoons milk
pinch of salt

Preheat the oven to 180°C/160°C fan/350°F/Gas Mark 4. Lightly grease a couple of baking sheets with a little butter.

Peel the banana and place in a food processor with the dates. Process for 4–5 seconds until the dates are in small pieces and the banana has become mashed, though your mixture should still have some texture (you don't want a purée).

Place the flour in a bowl, add the butter and rub in with your fingertips until the mixture resembles breadcrumbs. Add the date mixture, walnuts, milk and salt and stir everything together.

Use a tablespoon to place the mixture in 12 dollops on the baking sheets, spaced well apart. Use the back of the spoon to smear the dollops into rough rounds about 7cm (3 inches) in diameter and about 5mm (¼ inch) thick (if you want neat rounds, use a cookie cutter as a guide).

Bake the cookies for 20–25 minutes until the edges have become browned and hard, but the centres are still a little soft. Leave to cool on a wire rack and then store in an airtight container. They will keep for 2–3 days.

A combination of dried figs and whole almonds lends an attractive mosaic-like effect to these vanilla-flavoured cookies. Try them alongside an espresso – they make a great alternative to sugary biscotti.

Almond & Fig Cookies

MAKES 25

100g (3½oz) plain flour
50g (2oz) ground almonds
75g (3oz) unsalted butter,
　chilled and cut into chunks,
　plus extra for greasing
1 egg, beaten
1 tablespoon stevia powder
　(see page 187)
1 teaspoon unsweetened vanilla
　extract
85g (3¼oz) dried figs, stalks
　removed and finely chopped
35g (1¼oz) whole almonds, roughly
　chopped

Place the flour, ground almonds and butter in a food processor and pulse until you have a mixture with the texture of coffee grounds.

....

Stir the egg, stevia powder and vanilla extract together in a small bowl. Pour the mixture into the food processor and then pulse until all the ingredients come together as a dough.

....

Remove the dough from the food processor and knead in the figs and almonds until well combined. Shape the dough into a rectangular block about 12 x 8cm (5 x 3¼ inches), and about 3.5cm (1½ inches) thick. Place it in the freezer for an hour until it has become firm.

....

Preheat the oven to 180°C/160°C fan/350°F/Gas Mark 4. Lightly grease a baking sheet with a little butter.

....

Remove the dough block from the freezer. Using a sharp knife, carefully cut the block into slices no more than 5mm (¼ inch) thick. You may need to use a slight sawing action in order to cut neatly through the figs.

....

Place the cookies on the baking sheet and bake for 15–20 minutes until lightly browned and hardened. Leave to cool on a wire rack, then store in an airtight tin. They will keep for up to a week.

Palmiers are swirly biscuits made from puff pastry. They look complicated to make, but in practice the process is pretty simple – just don't tell anyone else!

Chocolate Hazelnut Palmiers

MAKES 15

250g (8oz) ready-made puff pastry
50g (2oz) whole hazelnuts
2 teaspoons cocoa powder
2 teaspoons stevia powder
  (see page 187)
pinch of ground mixed spice
plain flour, for dusting
4 teaspoons unsalted butter, very
  soft, plus extra for greasing

Bring the pastry out of the refrigerator an hour before you want to use it to allow it to reach room temperature.

Preheat the oven to 200°C/180°C fan/400°F/Gas Mark 6. Lightly grease a baking sheet with a little butter.

Place the hazelnuts, cocoa powder, stevia powder and mixed spice in a food processor and pulse until you have a mixture with the texture of coffee grounds.

Roll out the pastry on a worktop well dusted with flour to a rectangle about 22 x 32cm (8¾ x 12½ inches), and about 2mm (¹⁄₁₆ inch) thick. Spread with 3 teaspoons of the butter. Sprinkle two-thirds of the nut mixture across.

With one long side nearest to you, imagine a vertical line down the centre of your pastry. Fold either end of the pastry in to meet down the centre, then spread the remaining butter across the resulting surface, followed by the rest of the nut mixture.

Fold each side in to meet down the centre again. Finally, fold the left side over the right. You will now have a long, flattened sausage of folded pastry. Trim the ends to neaten and then cut into slices about 1cm (½ inch) thick.

Lay the slices cut side up on the baking sheet, spacing them well apart as they will spread dramatically. Bake for 15–20 minutes until golden. Leave to cool on a wire rack. These are best eaten on the day they are made.

These voluminous scones are enriched with wholemeal flour and naturally sweetened with rice milk. When served with a dollop of cream and some balsamic vinegar-infused strawberries, they'll not only give you that sweet treat you've been craving, but will also keep hunger pangs at bay.

Strawberry Scones

MAKES 8

225g (7½oz) plain flour, plus extra
   for dusting
75g (3oz) wholemeal plain flour
1 tablespoon baking powder
50g (2oz) unsalted butter, chilled
   and cut into chunks, plus extra
   for greasing
125ml (4fl oz) rice milk
85ml (3¼fl oz) milk

For the topping
500g (1lb) fresh strawberries, hulled
   and thinly sliced
2 teaspoons balsamic vinegar
¼ teaspoon ground black pepper
300ml (½ pint) whipping cream

Preheat the oven to 220°C/200°C fan/425°F/Gas Mark 7. Lightly grease a baking sheet with a little butter.

Mix both flours and the baking powder together in a large bowl. Add the butter and rub in with your fingertips until the mixture resembles fine breadcrumbs (you can pulse the ingredients in a food processor instead, if you prefer). Pour in the rice milk and milk. Stir everything together, then get your hands in and knead the mixture into a dough.

Roll out the dough on a worktop well dusted with flour to a thickness of about 3cm (1¼ inches). Use a 6cm (2½-inch) cookie cutter to cut out 8 rounds, rerolling the trimmings as necessary, and place them on the baking sheet. Bake for 15 minutes until well risen and browned.

To make the topping, stir the strawberry slices, vinegar and pepper together in a saucepan over a medium heat for 5 minutes, taking care not to let the mixture boil. Once the strawberries have become softened and translucent and have released some of their juices, remove the pan from the heat and leave everything to cool. Whip the cream until it forms soft peaks.

Serve the scones cut in half, with each side topped by a dollop of whipped cream and a serving of the balsamic strawberries.

Cakes & Gateaux

In a very roundabout way, this cake was inspired by a recipe from British Michelin-starred chef Tom Kerridge. It uses tea to create an extra depth of flavour and a springy, moist texture. A wicked chocolate ganache finishes it off nicely.

Chocolate Tea Cake

MAKES ABOUT 12 SLICES

1 Earl Grey teabag
110g (3¾oz) pitted dried dates
75g (3oz) wholemeal plain flour
25g (1oz) cocoa powder
100g (3½oz) unsalted butter, very
    soft, plus extra for greasing
2 eggs
2 teaspoons baking powder
pinch of ground cloves
pinch of salt
50g (2oz) no-added-sugar plain
    dark chocolate, plus extra for
    decorating

Use the teabag to make a pot of tea, using about 150ml (¼ pint) boiling water and leaving it to brew for 5 minutes. Pour off the tea into a measuring jug, then soak the dates in 125ml (4fl oz) of the tea for at least 4 hours or overnight, reserving the remaining tea for the ganache.

When the dates are softened and have absorbed most of the tea, preheat the oven to 180°C/160°C fan/350°F/Gas Mark 4. Lightly grease a 22 x 11 x 7cm (8¾ x 4½ x 3-inch)/1kg (2lb) loaf tin with a little butter.

Place the soaked dates and the tea they were soaking in in a food processor and process until smooth. Add the flour, cocoa powder, butter, eggs, baking powder, cloves and salt and process for 3–4 seconds until everything has combined.

Scoop the cake mixture into the tin and smooth the top with a spatula. Bake for 30 minutes until well risen and an inserted skewer comes out clean. Leave to cool in the tin before removing and placing on a serving plate.

Meanwhile, make the ganache. Break up the chocolate into small pieces and place in a small saucepan with the reserved tea over a low heat until the chocolate has melted, then stir well. Pour into a bowl and chill in the refrigerator for 30 minutes until the mixture has set. Spread it on the cooled cake. Use a vegetable peeler to create curls of chocolate and sprinkle over the top of the ganache to decorate. Eat within 2–3 days.

For this naturally gluten-free cake I've used the sunny Mediterranean flavours of apricots, almonds and lemon. It uses store cupboard ingredients and its gentle fragrance and moist, chunky almonds help to make it a tempting prospect at any time of the year. Try it at tea time or as more of a dessert with a little crème fraîche.

Apricot & Lemon Cake

MAKES ABOUT 12 SLICES

250g (8oz) soft dried apricots
300g (10oz) whole almonds
500ml (17fl oz) boiling water
sunflower oil, for oiling
juice and zest of ½ unwaxed lemon,
   plus extra zest
4 eggs
2 teaspoons baking powder
pinch of salt
12 blanched almonds
3 tablespoons fresh orange juice
crème fraîche, to serve

Set side 75g (3oz) of the apricots. Place the remaining apricots in a bowl. Place the whole almonds in a separate bowl. Pour 250ml (8fl oz) boiling water into each bowl and leave to stand for 2 hours or overnight.

Preheat the oven to 180°C/fan 160°C/350°F/Gas Mark 4. Generously oil a 28cm (11-inch) springform tin and line the base with baking parchment. Finely chop the reserved apricots.

Drain the soaked almonds and apricots and place them in a food processor with the lemon juice and zest, eggs, baking powder and salt. Blend for about 1 minute until the almonds are finely minced. Stir in the chopped apricots, then transfer the mixture to the tin. Arrange the blanched almonds on top.

Bake for 30 minutes, then cover with foil, reduce the heat to 160°C/fan 140°C /325°F/Gas Mark 3 and bake for a further 10 minutes. An inserted skewer should come out clean.

Leave the cake to cool in the tin. Run a butter knife around the edge before unclipping the tin. Transfer to a serving plate. Drizzle the orange juice over the top and let stand for 10 minutes before serving with a little crème fraîche topped with lemon zest.

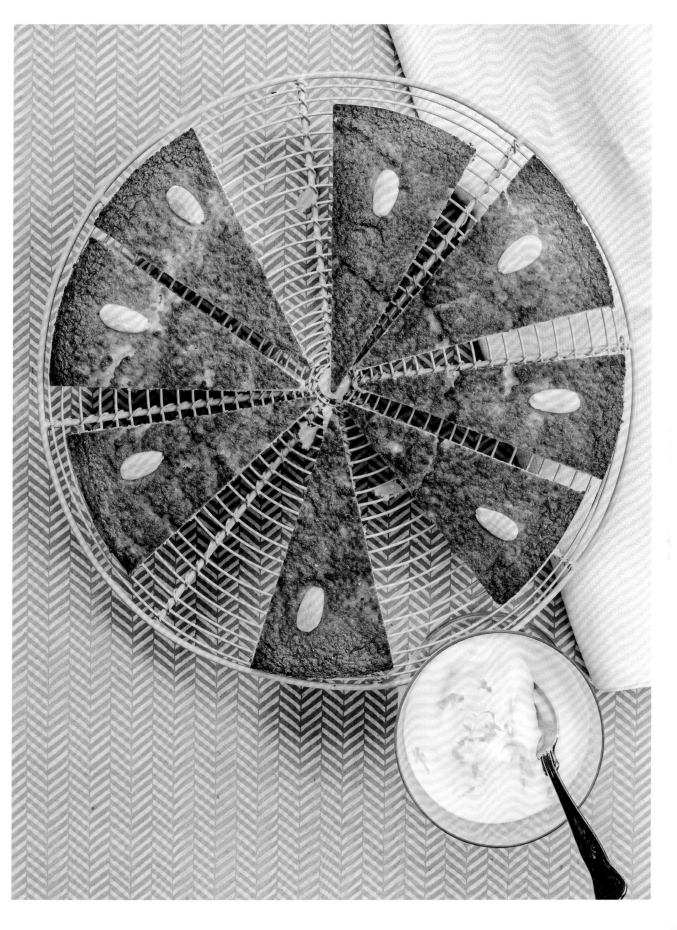

Flavours of treacle and toffee permeate this soft, super-moist cake. It is based on an Omani recipe, and though it is rather laden with dates, the small portion size keeps the sugar per slice to a minimum. I eat this cake cold as a mid-morning treat, but it would also be fabulous served warm with custard.

Sticky Date & Apple Cake

MAKES 25 PIECES

1 large dessert apple, about 200g (7oz), plus 1 extra, about 150g (5oz), for decorating

250g (8oz) pitted dried dates

250ml (8fl oz) water

100g (3½oz) unsalted butter, plus extra for greasing

1 teaspoon bicarbonate of soda

2 eggs

150g (5oz) wholemeal plain flour

2 teaspoons baking powder

1 teaspoon unsweetened vanilla extract

Preheat the oven to 200°C/180°C fan/400°F/Gas Mark 6. Lightly grease a 20cm (8-inch) square baking tin with a little butter.

Core the large apple (leave the skin on) and chop it roughly into pieces about 2.5cm (1 inch) in size. Place them in a saucepan with the dates and measurement water and bring to the boil. Boil the mixture for about 3 minutes until the apple is soft.

Meanwhile, quarter and core the smaller apple for decorating the cake (leave the skin), then cut it into thin slices and set aside.

Take the pan off the heat, then stir in the butter and allow it to melt. Next, stir in the bicarbonate of soda. It will foam up rather impressively.

Place the eggs, flour, baking powder and vanilla extract in a food processor. Add the foamy date mixture and blend for about 5 seconds until everything has combined.

Pour the cake mixture into the tin and gently smooth the top with a spatula. Arrange the sliced apple decoratively on top – I prefer a Modernist aesthetic, with the slices arranged in rows, but it's entirely up to you!

Bake for 40 minutes until the cake has risen and the edges are pulling away from the sides of the tin, and an inserted skewer comes out clean. Leave it to cool in the tin before cutting it into 25 pieces. Eat within 2–3 days.

Variation

You can easily make a dairy-free version of this cake by using dairy-free margarine in place of the butter.

This is a rich, moist fruit cake made using nutritious wholemeal flour, packed with raisins and apricots and topped with whole almonds.

Fruit Cake

MAKES 8 SLICES

50g (2oz) dried apricots, finely chopped
160g (5½oz) raisins
40g (1½oz) sultanas
2½ teaspoons ground mixed spice
grated rind and juice 1 large unwaxed orange
2 bananas, about 250g (8oz) total weight
50g (2oz) butter, softened, plus extra for greasing
100g (3½oz) wholemeal plain flour
50g (2oz) ground almonds
2 teaspoons baking powder
1 egg, beaten
75g (3oz) whole almonds

Preheat the oven to 160°C/140°C fan/325°F/Gas Mark 3. Lightly grease a deep 18cm (7-inch) round cake tin with a little butter, then place the tin on a sheet of baking paper and draw round it. Cut out the circle of baking paper and lay on the base of the tin.

Place all the dried fruit, mixed spice and orange rind in a bowl and stir to coat the fruit in the spice.

Peel and mash the bananas, then mix into the softened butter in a large bowl. Stir in the flour, ground almonds, baking powder and egg until you have a paste.

Make up the orange juice in a measuring jug to 125ml (4fl oz) with water if necessary and stir into the cake mixture. Now add the spiced fruit mixture and then stir well.

Scoop the cake mixture into the tin and smooth the top with a spatula. Use the whole almonds to decorate the top.

Bake for 1 hour 40 minutes (don't open the door!) until the cake is well browned and an inserted skewer comes out clean. Leave to cool in the tin, then run a butter knife around the edge before carefully turning the tin upside down to remove the cake. This cake is best eaten within a week.

Variation

Make this cake dairy free by using dairy-free margarine in place of the butter.

Tip

If you don't have any mixed spice, you can use a mixture of 1 teaspoon ground cinnamon, 1 teaspoon ground coriander, ¼ teaspoon ground nutmeg and ¼ teaspoon ground cloves instead.

The colourful nectarine slices are embedded within the soft vanilla sponge of this cake, making it not only attractive but also providing a lovely burst of sweetness. This cake works well both warm or cold, and if you want to make it more of a dessert, try it with some of my Vanilla Ice Cream (see page 89).

Nectarine Upside Down Cake

MAKES ABOUT 8 SLICES

75g (3oz) soft dried apricots
2 fresh nectarines
100g (3½oz) plain flour
75g (3oz) ground almonds
150g (5oz) unsalted butter, very soft, plus extra for greasing
2 teaspoons baking powder
1 teaspoon unsweetened vanilla extract
4 eggs
1 teaspoon ground cinnamon, plus extra for dusting

Place the dried apricots in a mug and cover with boiling water. Leave them to soak for about 15 minutes.

Meanwhile, preheat the oven to 180°C/160°C fan/350°F/Gas Mark 4. Lightly grease a 20cm (8-inch) springform tin with a little butter.

Working over a bowl to catch the juice, slice the nectarines in half and remove the stone, then cut each half into about 8 segments. Arrange the segments decoratively across the base of the cake tin, aiming to cover as much of it as possible.

Drain the soaked dried apricots and place them in a food processor with all the remaining ingredients, including any juice reserved from preparing the nectarines. Process the mixture for about 10–15 seconds until you have a smooth cake mixture. Pour it on top of the nectarine slices and gently smooth the top with a spatula.

Bake the cake for 30 minutes until risen and golden brown, and an inserted skewer comes out clean. Leave the cake to cool in the tin for about 5 minutes, then run a butter knife around the outside of the cake, place an upturned serving plate on top and carefully flip both over together. Remove the tin to reveal your cake. Dust it with cinnamon to serve. Store the finished cake in the refrigerator and eat within a couple of days – it actually tastes better a day after it is made.

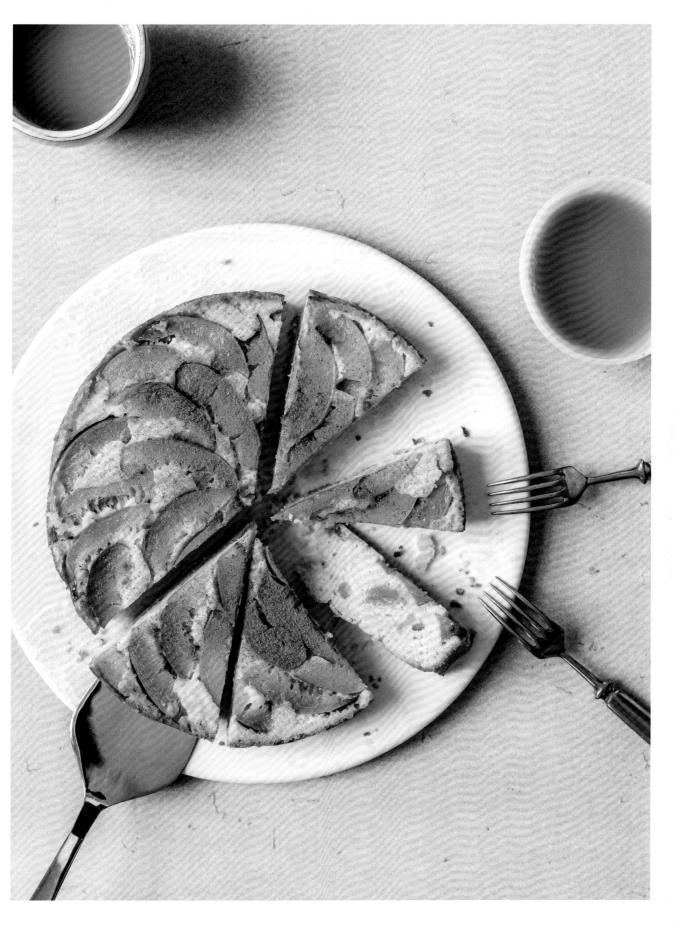

This is goodness in cake form, packed with butternut squash, dates and apricots. It tastes best the day after it is made, so it's perfect for when you want to get your baking done in advance.

Spicy Ginger Cake with Apricot Topping

MAKES 16 SQUARES

For the cake
150g (5oz) butternut squash
2 teaspoons sunflower oil, plus extra
    for oiling
75g (3oz) unsalted butter, melted
100g (3½oz) pitted dried dates
125ml (4fl oz) milk
2 teaspoons ground ginger
1 teaspoon ground cinnamon
grated rind of 1 large unwaxed
    orange
200g (7oz) plain flour
2 teaspoons baking powder
1 egg, beaten

For the topping
50g (2oz) unsweetened smooth
    cashew nut butter
25g (1oz) salted butter, very soft
75g (3oz) soft dried apricots, finely
    chopped
15g (½oz) raw unsalted cashew
    nuts, finely chopped

Preheat the oven to 200°C/180°C fan/400°F/Gas Mark 6. Lightly oil a 20cm (8-inch) square tin with a little sunflower oil.

Deseed the butternut squash (keep the skin on) and cut into pieces about 1cm (½ inch) square, then toss them in the oil in a roasting tin. Roast for 20 minutes until cooked through but only just browned. Remove them from the oven and leave to cool for about 5 minutes.

Place the roasted squash in a food processor with the melted butter, dates, milk, spices and orange rind. Process until nearly smooth. Stir in the flour, baking powder and egg.

Transfer the mixture to the tin, smooth the top with a spatula and bake for 20–30 minutes. Leave to cool in the tin.

To make the topping, beat the cashew nut butter and butter together. Spread the mixture across the top of the cooled cake, then sprinkle the apricot and cashews across the nut paste. Chill the cake in the refrigerator for an hour until the topping has set, then cut into 16 squares. This cake will keep for 2–3 days.

Variation

Use dairy-free margarine in place of butter and soya milk in place of milk to create a dairy-free version of this recipe.

This is a fabulously moist, spiced carrot cake, with natural sweetness provided not only by the carrot and raisins but also by the generous quantity of dreamy, orange-flavoured frosting.

Carrot Cake

MAKES ABOUT 12 SLICES

For the cake
150g (5oz) walnuts, chopped
250g (8oz) carrot, peeled and finely grated
150g (5oz) wholemeal plain flour
2 teaspoons ground cinnamon
¼ teaspoon ground cloves
2 teaspoons baking powder
½ teaspoon bicarbonate of soda
125ml (4fl oz) sunflower oil, plus extra for oiling
250ml (8fl oz) milk
2 eggs, beaten
2 tablespoons stevia powder (see page 187)
1 tablespoon fresh orange juice
75g (3oz) sultanas

For the frosting
85ml (3¼fl oz) whipping cream
140g (4½oz) cream cheese
1 tablespoon stevia powder (see page 187)
1 tablespoon fresh orange juice
grated rind of 1 unwaxed orange, plus extra for decorating
2 tablespoons chopped walnuts

Preheat the oven to 180°C/160°C fan/350°F/Gas Mark 4. Lightly oil a 22 x 11 x 7cm (8¾ x 4½ x 3-inch)/1kg (2lb) loaf tin with a little sunflower oil.

Place 100g (3½oz) of the walnut pieces in a food processor and process them to the texture of coarse coffee grounds. Transfer to a bowl and add the grated carrot, flour, spices, baking powder and bicarbonate of soda. Give everything a good stir.

Mix the oil, milk, eggs, stevia powder and orange juice together in a jug. Pour the liquid mixture into the bowl with the other ingredients and stir quickly until everything is combined. Add the sultanas and remainder of the walnuts, give another quick stir and then pour the cake mixture into the loaf tin. Smooth the top with a spatula.

Bake the loaf for 45–50 minutes until browned and risen, and an inserted skewer comes out clean. Leave the cake to cool in the tin.

To make the frosting, whip the cream until it forms soft peaks and then beat in the cream cheese. Stir the stevia powder into the orange juice in a jug until it has dissolved and then pour it into the cream cheese mixture. Add the grated rind and fold everything together with a spatula.

Remove the cake from the tin. Smear the cream cheese mixture across the top, then use a fork to make a decorative pattern. Finish by scattering the chopped walnuts across the top, along with a little extra grated rind. Store the finished cake in the refrigerator and eat within a couple of days.

Gateau Marcel is a two-tier chocolate mousse, one raw and one baked into a soft cake. Invented by the Michelin-starred chef Michel Michaud, this indulgent and gluten-free creation is easy to make, although it does need to be prepared in advance.

Gateau Marcel with Cherries & Blueberries

SERVES 6–8

sunflower oil, for oiling
100g (3½oz) no-added-sugar plain dark chocolate, broken into small pieces
50g (2oz) no-added-sugar milk chocolate, broken into small pieces
150g (5oz) unsalted butter, chopped
pinch of fine salt
2 eggs
3 egg whites
150g (5oz) fresh black cherries, pitted and halved
75g (3oz) fresh blueberries

Preheat the oven to 180°C/160°C fan/350°F/Gas Mark 4. Line the base of a 20cm (8-inch) square cake tin with baking paper and lightly oil the sides with a little sunflower oil.

Place the chocolates and butter with the salt in a saucepan over a low heat until they have melted, stirring occasionally.

Separate the whole eggs. Place all the whites in a medium bowl and the yolks in a large bowl.

Using an electric whisk, whisk the whites until very stiff – you will have reached the right level of stiffness if they won't move when the bowl is tipped to the side.

Use the whisk to whisk the yolks until they have turned a few shades paler and become fluffy. While continuing to whisk, very slowly pour in the hot chocolate mixture in a thin stream. You'll be left with a thick and glossy chocolate paste.

Fold the whisked egg whites into the chocolate paste. When everything has been combined and you have a mousse, pour half the mixture into the cake tin. Bake for 20 minutes until puffy.

Leave the cake to cool in the tin (it will sink significantly), then pour the remaining chocolate mousse on top of the cake. Place in the refrigerator for at least 4 hours until set.

When you are ready to serve, run a butter knife around the edge of the gateau and lift it out of the tin. Remove the lining paper. Place the gateau on a serving plate. Scatter the cherries and blueberries across the top of the gateau.

Tip

If you have egg yolks left over after making this recipe, consider using them to make the Portuguese Custard Tarts (see page 58), Vanilla Ice Cream (see page 89) or Chocolate Chip Ice Cream (see page 89).

There's a hint of tiramisu flavouring in this light sponge cake, which is filled with a rich and creamy chestnut and prune centre. A dusting of cocoa finishes everything off nicely.

Chestnut Tiramisu Cake

SERVES 8–12

For the sponge
sunflower oil, for oiling
6 eggs
125g (4oz) chestnut flour
pinch of salt
4 tablespoons freshly made strong
    coffee, cooled
2 tablespoons white rum (optional)

For the filling and decoration
100g (3½oz) pitted prunes
85ml (3¼fl oz) boiling water
2 teaspoons unsweetened vanilla
    extract
2 teaspoons stevia powder (see
    page 187)
375ml (13fl oz) whipping cream
200g (7oz) unsweetened chestnut
    purée
2 teaspoons cocoa powder, for
    dusting

Before you start, soak the prunes for the filling and decoration in the measurement boiling water, ideally for a minimum of 2 hours.

Preheat the oven to 180°C/160°C fan/350°F/Gas Mark 4. Lightly oil two 20cm (8-inch) sandwich tins with a little sunflower oil, then place one tin on a double-thickness sheet of baking paper and draw round it. Cut out the circles of baking paper and lay one on the base of each tin.

To make the sponge, separate the eggs and place the whites in a large bowl and the yolks in a separate bowl.

Using an electric whisk, whisk the whites until very stiff – they shouldn't move when the bowl is tipped to the side.

Whisk the yolks until they have turned a few shades paler and become fluffy. Fold into the whisked egg white, followed by the chestnut flour and salt.

When everything is well combined, divide the mixture between the tins and bake for 15 minutes until just browned. Leave the sponges to cool in the tins.

For the filling, place the softened prunes and their soaking water in a blender and blend to a purée, then set aside.

Stir the vanilla extract and stevia powder together in a jug until the stevia has dissolved. Pour into a large bowl with the cream. Whip the cream until it forms firm peaks, then fold in the chestnut purée.

Now it's time to assemble your cake. Place the first sponge layer on a serving plate. Stir the coffee and rum together, if using. Pour half across the sponge layer, followed by one-third of the cream mixture, spreading it evenly across the sponge base. Spread the prune purée on top.

Add the second sponge layer and drench it with the remaining coffee mixture, followed by a further one-third of the cream. Pipe the remaining cream around the sides of the cake. Dust the top with the cocoa powder and serve. Store in the refrigerator and eat within a couple of days.

This German-style cake is topped with juicy pears and flaked almonds. I've used canned pears for ease, but peeled, ripe dessert pears would make a wonderful alternative.

Pear Kuchen

MAKES 9 PIECES

125ml (4fl oz) milk, plus
   1 tablespoon for glazing
1 teaspoon unsweetened vanilla
   extract
1 tablespoon stevia powder (see
   page 187)
25g (1oz) salted butter, chopped,
   plus extra for greasing
1 teaspoon fast-action dried yeast
150g (5oz) plain flour
50g (2oz) ground almonds
1 egg, beaten
225g (7½oz) drained canned pear
   halves in fruit juice
1 tablespoon flaked almonds

Lightly grease a 20cm (8-inch) square cake tin with a little butter.

Heat the milk with the vanilla extract and stevia powder in a saucepan. Just before it starts to boil, take the pan off the heat, add the butter and leave it to melt. When the liquid has cooled to hand-hot, stir in the yeast.

Mix the flour and ground almonds together in a bowl. Pour the milk mixture and egg into the bowl, and stir to combine everything into a soft, sticky dough.

Press the dough into the tin, using the back of a spoon to ease it into the corners and to create an even layer. Leave it under a clean damp tea towel somewhere warm for an hour or so until it looks puffy.

Preheat the oven to 200°C/180°C fan/400°F/Gas Mark 6. Cut each pear half into 6 slices and arrange them on the top of the dough. Brush all the exposed dough with the remaining tablespoon of milk and sprinkle over the flaked almonds.

Bake for 25 minutes until the dough has risen and become golden. Cut into 9 pieces, then leave to cool for a while in the tin and serve warm. This is best eaten the same day.

I love the dramatic colour contrast of red velvet cake and this recipe gives a moist and moreish result, yet it's packed with goodness, so different from shop-bought versions! Of course, no red velvet cake would be worth its name without a wicked cream cheese frosting, so there is plenty of that too.

Red Velvet Cake

SERVES 8–12

For the cake
250g (8oz) fresh beetroot
150g (5oz) wholemeal plain flour
150g (5oz) white plain flour
4 teaspoons baking powder
1 tablespoon cocoa powder
250ml (8fl oz) sunflower oil, plus extra for oiling
175ml (6fl oz) milk
85ml (3¼fl oz) natural yogurt
4 tablespoons freshly made strong coffee, cooled
2 eggs
4 tablespoons stevia powder (see page 187)
2 teaspoons unsweetened vanilla extract
2 teaspoons red food colouring (optional)
1 teaspoon balsamic vinegar

For the frosting
375ml (13fl oz) whipping cream
150g (5oz) cream cheese
3 teaspoons unsweetened vanilla extract
2 tablespoons stevia powder (see page 187)

Preheat the oven to 180°C/160°C fan/350°F/Gas Mark 4. Lightly oil two 20cm (8-inch) sandwich tins with a little sunflower oil and line the bases with nonstick baking paper.

Finely grate the beetroot into a large bowl and add both flours, the baking powder and cocoa powder. Mix all the remaining cake ingredients together in a separate bowl or jug. Pour the liquid mixture into the beetroot mixture and stir quickly until you have a sloppy pink mixture. Divide it evenly between the cake tins.

Bake the cakes for 40 minutes until risen and browned, and an inserted skewer comes out clean. Remove the cakes from their tins and leave them to cool upside down on a wire rack.

To make the frosting, whip the cream until it forms soft peaks, then whisk in the cream cheese. Stir the vanilla extract and stevia powder together until the stevia has dissolved, then add to the cream cheese mixture. Whip briefly until everything is combined.

To assemble the cake, place the first cake layer on a serving plate and spread half the frosting across it. Add the second cake layer, followed by the remaining frosting. Use a fork to add a few decorative swirls to the frosting. Keep the finished cake in the refrigerator until ready to serve. Eat within a couple of days.

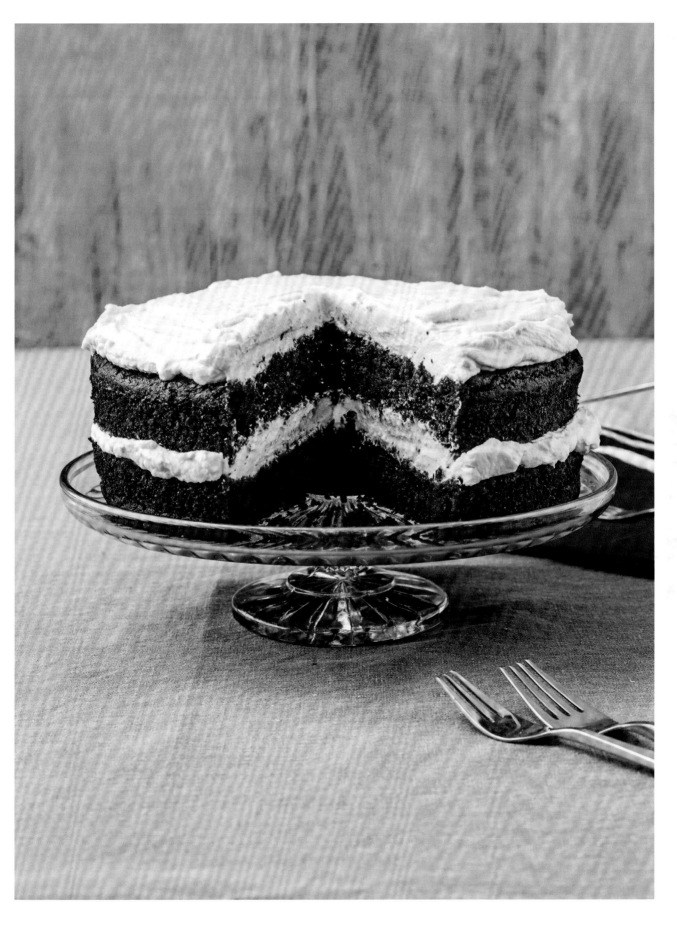

These tarts are known as pasteis de nata and I became familiar with them after living in London's 'little Portugal' district. They can be tricky to make at home (the recipe originates from a Lisbon café that has an extremely hot oven), but by using my technique it is possible to achieve great results.

Portuguese Custard Tarts

MAKES 12

butter, for greasing
300g (10oz) ready-made puff pastry
85ml (3¼fl oz) milk
1 tablespoon plain flour, plus extra for dusting
2 egg yolks
2 eggs, beaten
175ml (6fl oz) rice milk
2 teaspoons stevia powder (see page 187)
1 teaspoon unsweetened vanilla extract
½ teaspoon ground cinnamon, for dusting

Tip
If you have egg whites left over, why not use them to make my Gateau Marcel (see page 53)?

Bring the pastry out of the refrigerator an hour before you want to use it to allow it to reach room temperature.

Preheat the oven to 240°C/220°C fan/475°F/Gas Mark 9. Grease the cups of a 12-cup muffin tin with butter.

Roll out the pastry on a worktop well dusted with flour to a rectangle about 17 x 12cm (6¾ x 5 inches), and about 1cm (½ inch) thick, but don't worry if you accidentally make it a little larger than this. Brush the top with water and then, starting from one short side, roll it up tightly. You'll now have a cylinder of pastry.

Trim the ends of the pastry cylinder to neaten it, then cut it into 4 equal lengths and cut each length into 3 slices. With the cut side uppermost, roll your rolling pin over each slice a couple of times so that you get a rough round about 7cm (3 inches) in diameter. Place a pastry round into each cup of the muffin tin and use your fingertips to stretch the pastry until you have lined each cup and there are no gaps.

For the filling, stir the milk and flour together in a bowl until smooth. Beat the egg yolks and whole eggs together in a separate bowl and set 1 tablespoon aside. Pour the remaining egg into the milk. Add the rice milk, stevia powder and vanilla extract and whisk until everything is combined.

Pour the filling into the pastry cases, dividing the mixture evenly between them. Brush the exposed pastry with the reserved egg.

Bake the custard tarts for 15 minutes until the filling has risen and has brown spots. Leave the tarts to cool in the tin for about 10 minutes – the filling will sink down as they do so. Dust a little of the cinnamon over each one and then serve. These are best eaten the same day.

These simple fruit tarts are fresh and easy, and are a great idea for an elegant event – scattered with edible flowers, they'll easily be the star attraction.

Raspberry Tarts

MAKES 4

sunflower oil, for oiling
plain flour, for dusting
1 quantity of Low-carb Dessert
  Pastry (see page 170)
125ml (4fl oz) whipping cream
1 large ripe dessert pear, about
  175g (6oz), peeled and cored
275g (9oz) fresh raspberries
handful of edible flower petals, such
  as viola or dianthus (optional)

Preheat the oven to 200°C/180°C fan/400°F/Gas Mark 6. Lightly oil four 10cm (4-inch) round fluted tart tins with a little sunflower oil.

Roll out the pastry on a worktop well dusted with flour to a thickness of about 3–4mm (about ⅛ inch). Roughly cut out 4 rounds slightly larger than the tins. Press each pastry round into a tin and trim the excess with a sharp knife.

Place a layer of foil over the top of each pastry case, then fill with dried beans or baking beans. Bake for 20 minutes until the pastry is crisp and just turning golden brown. Leave the pastry cases to cool in the tins and then lift the beans and foil out.

Just before you want to serve your tarts, remove the pastry cases from the tins and place them on a serving plate. Whip the cream until it forms soft peaks. Place the pear in a separate bowl and use a stick blender to purée it, then fold it into the cream. Spread the cream mixture evenly across each of the tarts and arrange the raspberries on top. Finish with a scattering of edible flower petals, if you like. These are best eaten immediately.

Desserts

This sunset-coloured jelly is made with fresh juices and studded with pomegranate seeds. Serve with cream or my Vanilla Ice Cream (see page 89).

Clementine & Pomegranate Jelly

SERVES 4

10 clementines, about 750g (1½lb) total weight
2 pomegranates
2 tablespoons white wine
5 leaves of gelatine

First, thoroughly juice the clementines into a measuring jug and set aside. Pomegranates can be messy, but there is a simple way to extract the juice. Score a line all the way round each pomegranate with a knife. Now score a second line at a right angle to the first. Fill a large bowl with water and hold one pomegranate underneath the water. Pull it apart along the scored lines, then loosen all the seeds. The white pith should float to the surface while the seeds sink. Using a slotted spoon, fish out as much of the pith as you can, then pour the contents of the bowl through a colander. You will be left with the seeds. Repeat the process for the second pomegranate. Take one-quarter of the seeds and scatter them in the base of a 600ml (1-pint) jelly mould or 4 individual 150ml (¼ pint) jelly moulds.

Place the remaining pomegranate seeds in a plastic tub. Using the back of a tablespoon, press down on each seed until it is squashed flat and the juice has come out. Strain the mixture through a sieve into the clementine juice. You will now have a beautiful pinkish orange liquid. Add the wine and, if necessary, make up the quantity of liquid to 500ml (17fl oz) with water.

Place the leaves of gelatine in a bowl and cover with cold water. Leave to soak for 5 minutes so that they become really floppy, then transfer them to a small saucepan and heat very gently until they melt. Add the juice to the pan and stir until everything is combined.

Pour the juice mixture into the jelly mould and refrigerate overnight.

To serve, place the mould in a bowl of hand-hot water (don't let the water come over the sides of the jelly mould) until the edges of the jelly have melted very slightly. This will happen very quickly for metal moulds, but will be slower with plastic moulds. Place an upturned serving dish on top of the mould, then flip both over together, give a quick shake and remove the mould. Serve immediately.

Variation

To make a vegetarian/vegan version of this recipe, stir 1 tablespoon agar powder (see page 186) into 4 tablespoons of the clementine juice in a small saucepan and heat gently until it has dissolved. Pour in the remaining liquid (make sure the wine is suitable for vegans, if necessary) and make up to 500ml (17fl oz) with water if necessary. Pour the juice mixture into the mould with the pomegranate seeds as detailed above, then chill in the refrigerator for a couple of hours before serving.

Crisp, fresh red grapes are the secret to this tart's success –
not only are they a wonderful counterbalance to the seductive
chocolate filling, they also give the tart its distinctive jewel-like
appearance. This tastes great served with cream.

Jewelled Chocolate Tart

SERVES 6–8

butter, for greasing
plain flour, for dusting
1 quantity of Low-carb Dessert
    Pastry (see page 170)
150g (5oz) no-added-sugar plain
    dark chocolate, broken into small
    pieces
185ml (6½fl oz) double cream
4 eggs
300g (10oz) red seedless grapes
1 teaspoon red wine
½ teaspoon raw local honey

Preheat the oven to 200°C/180°C fan/400°F/Gas Mark 6. Lightly grease
a 20cm (8-inch) tart tin with a little butter.

Roll out the pastry on a worktop well dusted with flour to a thickness of
about 3mm (⅛ inch). Roughly cut out a round slightly larger than the tin.
Press the pastry into the tin and trim the excess with a sharp knife. Set the
pastry case aside.

Place the chocolate with the cream in a saucepan over a low heat until
it has melted, stirring occasionally. Whisk the eggs together in a bowl for
8–10 minutes until doubled in volume and pale in colour. While continuing
to whisk, very slowly pour in the hot chocolate mixture in a thin stream.
You will end up with a dark chocolaty custard. Pour it into the pastry case.

Bake the tart for 40–45 minutes until the filling has puffed up all over and
taken on a cracked appearance. Remove from the oven.

While the tart cools a little, use kitchen paper to polish the grapes and
remove the bloom. Slice the grapes in half. I like to slice some vertically
and some horizontally to give greater scope for creativity in decorating
the tart. Arrange the grapes in concentric circles across the top of the
chocolate filling.

Stir the wine and honey together in a cup to create a glaze. Brush the
grapes with the red wine mixture and then serve immediately.

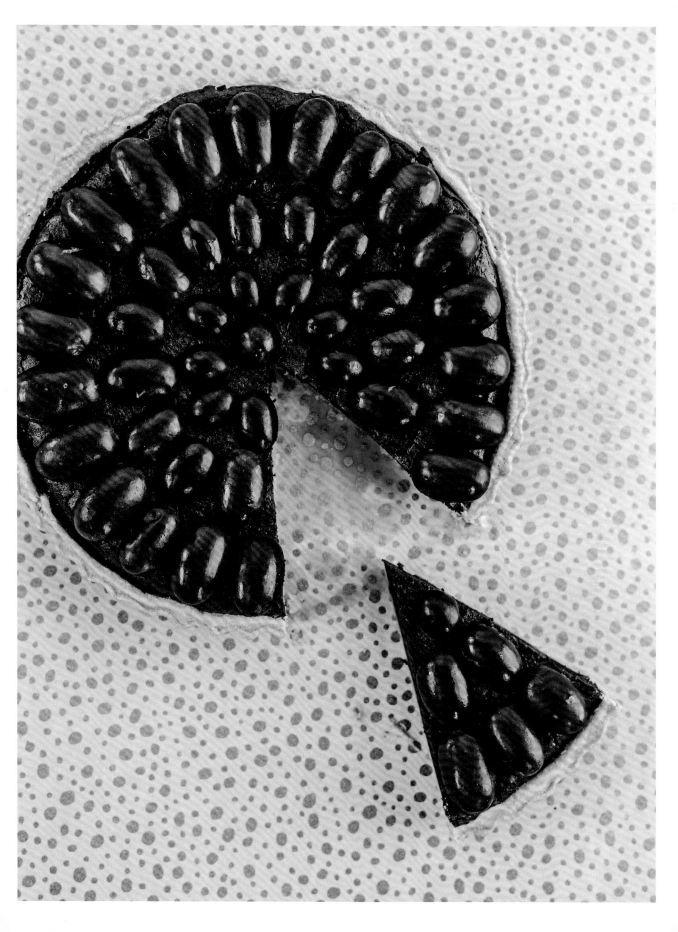

Evaporated milk is a very underrated ingredient with a distinctive flavour and delicate sweetness. It goes brilliantly with cream cheese and mandarin oranges in this retro chilled cheesecake. If you can't find oatcakes, use wholemeal savoury crackers instead.

Mandarin Cheesecake

SERVES 6–8

For the base

125g (4oz) unsweetened oatcakes

50g (2oz) unsalted butter, melted

2 teaspoons stevia powder (see page 187)

½ teaspoon ground ginger

For the topping

3 leaves of gelatine

250ml (8fl oz) whipping cream

250g (8oz) cream cheese

85ml (3¼fl oz) evaporated milk

1 teaspoon stevia powder (see page 187)

2 x 300g (10oz) cans mandarin orange segments in juice

Bash the oatcakes into crumbs by placing them in a sealed plastic food bag and hitting with a rolling pin. Alternatively, blitz them in a food processor. Stir the melted butter into the crumb mixture with the stevia powder and ginger. Tip the crumb mixture into a deep 20cm (8-inch) loose-bottomed flan tin and then use the back of a metal tablespoon to gently stroke the mixture until it is smooth and evenly distributed. Chill in the refrigerator for at least an hour until the butter has set.

To make the topping, place the leaves of gelatine in a bowl and cover with cold water. Leave to soak for 5 minutes so that they become really floppy. Meanwhile, whip the cream until it forms firm peaks. Add the cream cheese, evaporated milk and stevia powder and whip until you have a smooth, somewhat sloppy mixture.

Drain one can of mandarin segments and place 4 tablespoons of the juice in a small saucepan. Add the softened gelatine leaves and heat very gently until they melt. Pour the gelatine mixture into the cream cheese mixture and whip briefly. Pour on to the prepared biscuit base and put the tin back in the refrigerator for at least 2 hours.

Just before serving, drain the second can of mandarin segments. Decoratively arrange the segments from both cans on the top of the cheesecake. Release the cheesecake from the tin and serve.

Variation

Use gluten-free crackers for a gluten-free version of this dessert.

This chilled dessert combines a variety of Mediterranean flavours in an unusual yet delightful way. I tried something similar in a Copenhagen restaurant some years ago and totally fell in love with it. The almond rice is gently sweetened with rice milk, while the balsamic figs give an amazing burst of flavour – but do start soaking them the day before, if you can.

Creamy Almond Rice with Balsamic Figs

SERVES 4–6

For the balsamic figs
200g (7oz) soft dried figs
175ml (6fl oz) boiling water
1 tablespoon balsamic vinegar

For the almond rice
100g (3½oz) short-grain rice
500ml (17fl oz) rice milk
2 tablespoons sherry or vermouth
375ml (13fl oz) whipping cream
110g (3¾oz) whole blanched
  almonds, finely chopped

Remove the tough stalky part at the top of each fig, then cut each fig into 5 or 6 slices and place in a bowl with the measurement boiling water and balsamic vinegar. Leave to soak for at least 4 hours, or preferably overnight.

....

Place the rice and rice milk in a saucepan and bring to the boil, then reduce the heat and simmer for about 15 minutes until the rice is tender and almost all the liquid has been absorbed. Stir in the sherry or vermouth, then leave the mixture to cool completely. It will become really stodgy and rather solid, but this is fine.

....

Whip the cream until it forms firm peaks. Add to the cooled rice with the almonds and fold everything together until well combined. Serve each portion of almond rice topped with the balsamic figs.

These pears not only turn a dark pink during their gentle poaching in spiced wine but also take on a buttery smoothness. They are fantastic eaten with the cool and creamy mascarpone. This dish works best with slightly underripe pears of an even shape and size. Serve hot or cold.

Poached Pears with Mascarpone

SERVES 4

4 firm Conference pears, about
175g (6oz) each
250ml (8fl oz) red wine
250ml (8fl oz) water
1 cinnamon stick
4 cloves
grated rind of ½ unwaxed lemon
250ml (8fl oz) mascarpone cheese

For the sauce
1 ripe pear
1 teaspoon cornflour
2 teaspoons water

Peel the 4 pears but leave them whole. Lay them sideways in a deep 16cm (6¼-inch) pan – it will be a bit of a squeeze, but they should all fit in. Pour over the wine and measurement water until the pears are nearly submerged. Add the whole spices and lemon rind.

Heat the pears over a low heat for 40 minutes. After about 20 minutes, use a spoon to turn the pears gently to ensure even coloration. Strain the liquid from the pears into a bowl, then reserve 125ml (4fl oz) of it and discard the rest along with the spices.

To make the sauce, peel the pear and remove the core. Place in a blender with the reserved poaching liquid and blend to a purée. Strain the purée through a sieve into a saucepan over a low heat.

Mix the cornflour with the measurement water in a cup until smooth. Stir into the wine and pear mixture, then heat gently, stirring continuously, until boiling and thickened.

Cut a sliver off the base of each whole pear to enable them to sit upright on their serving plate. Finish by adding a dollop of the mascarpone, surrounded by a swirl of the sauce.

Variation

Serve with soya cream in place of the mascarpone to make this recipe vegan and dairy free.

The fruitiness of the prunes lends an extra dimension to the flavour of the chocolate, meaning this irresistible mousse is rich in taste yet has a wonderfully light consistency. Serve in elegant stemmed glasses to make it extra special.

Chocolate Mousse

SERVES 4

100g (3½oz) pitted prunes
4 tablespoons water
3 teaspoons amaretto
25g (1oz) no-added-sugar plain
   dark chocolate, broken into small
   pieces, plus extra for decorating
125ml (4fl oz) soured cream
25g (1oz) cocoa powder
4 egg whites
pinch of salt

Soak the prunes in the measurement water and amaretto for about 4 hours. After this time, strain any remaining liquid into a small saucepan and add the chocolate. Stir gently over a low heat until the chocolate has melted.

Place the prunes, melted chocolate mixture, soured cream and cocoa powder in a blender and blend until you have a thick, smooth paste. Transfer it to a large bowl.

Using an electric whisk, whisk the egg whites with the salt until very stiff – you will have reached the right level of stiffness if they won't move when the bowl is tipped to the side. Gently fold into the chocolate prune mixture until everything is evenly combined.

Divide the mixture between 4 dessert glasses. Smooth the top of each portion using a butter knife. Finally, grate a little extra chocolate over the top. Chill in the refrigerator for at least an hour before serving.

Variation

For a different slant on this recipe and to make it nut-free, use whisky in place of the amaretto.

Thinly sliced apples, fried in butter, are then cooked in a whisky-flavoured almond batter – basically, it's a dessert version of the classic Spanish tortilla. Serve it hot, with crème fraîche or my Vanilla Ice Cream (see page 89).

Apple Tortilla

SERVES 4

4 dessert apples, about 625g (1¼lb) total weight
25g (1oz) unsalted butter
4 eggs
50g (2oz) ground almonds
4 tablespoons soured cream
4 tablespoons milk
2 tablespoons whisky
2 teaspoons stevia powder (see page 187)
½ teaspoon unsweetened vanilla extract

Cut the apples into quarters, remove the cores (leave the skin on) and then slice them very thinly. Melt the butter in a 30cm (12-inch) frying pan and fry the apple slices over a low heat, to prevent them burning, for about 10 minutes until soft.

Meanwhile, whisk all the remaining ingredients together in a bowl. Pour the mixture over the softened apples and then leave the pan on a medium to medium-low heat for about 30 minutes until the surface of the mixture loses its gloss and has set. Cut the tortilla into slices and serve immediately.

A roulade is not difficult to make but always looks impressive, so it's a win-win situation. This one is filled with cream sweetened with banana, while passion fruit adds a zingy, acidic bite that totally lifts the overall dessert.

Tropical Roulade

SERVES 8

For the sponge
1 banana, about 200g (7oz)
4 eggs
100g (3½oz) plain flour

For the filling
300ml (½ pint) whipping cream
2 bananas, about 400g (13oz) total weight
6 passion fruit

Preheat the oven to 220°C/200°C fan/425°F/Gas Mark 7. Line a 36 x 28cm (14 x 11-inch) baking tin with silicone baking paper.

Peel and mash the banana in a large bowl. Separate the eggs and add the yolks to the banana and place the whites in a medium bowl. Using an electric whisk, whisk the egg whites until very stiff – you will have reached the right level of stiffness if they won't move when the bowl is tipped to the side.

Whisk the yolks and banana together until you have a foamy mixture. Sift the flour on top of the yolks, then spoon the whisked whites on top of the flour. Gently fold everything together until well combined.

Gently spread the mixture evenly across the baking paper in the baking tin. Bake for 10 minutes until golden brown. Lift the sponge out of the baking tin using the lining paper. With the paper still in place and using a clean tea towel to hold the sponge, roll it up, starting from one short edge, into a cylinder. Leave it to cool completely.

Just before you want to eat, make the filling. Whip the cream until it forms firm peaks. Peel and mash one of the bananas, then fold into the cream. Peel and finely slice the second banana. Cut the passion fruit in half and scoop out the seeds and pulp. Reserve some of the fruit for decoration. Gently unroll the sponge cylinder and spread it with two-thirds of the cream mixture. Scatter the banana slices and passion fruit seeds and pulp across the cream. Roll the sponge up again, gently peeling off the lining paper as you do so.

Place the finished roulade seam down and trim the ends to neaten it. Spread the the top with the remaining cream mixture. Top with the reserved banana and passion fruit. Cut it into slices and serve immediately.

Ripe, juicy plums have a wonderful natural sweetness that marries well with the toasted almonds and cinnamon in these simple tarts. Serve with whipped cream or crème fraîche.

Plum Tarts

MAKES 6

150g (5oz) ready-made puff pastry
sunflower oil, for oiling
plain flour, for dusting
3 teaspoons milk
25g (1oz) flaked almonds
4 ripe plums, about 250g (8oz) total weight
½ teaspoon ground cinnamon

Bring the pastry out of the refrigerator an hour before you want to use it to allow it to reach room temperature.

Preheat the oven to 200°C/180°C fan/400°F/Gas Mark 6. Lightly oil a baking sheet with a little sunflower oil.

Roll out the pastry on a worktop well dusted with flour to a thickness of about 3mm (⅛ inch). Use a 9cm (3½-inch) round pastry cutter, or the top of a mug or similar as a guide, to cut out 6 rounds and place them on the baking sheet, rerolling the trimmings as necessary. Use a slightly smaller cutter, or mug, about 6cm (2½ inches) in diameter, and lightly press it into the centre of each of your pastry rounds without cutting all the way through the pastry. Bake for 15 minutes until puffed and golden.

While the pastry is baking, toast the almonds in a dry frying pan until browned. Cut the plums in half and remove the stones, then chop the plums into small pieces, about 1cm (½ inch) in size.

Remove the pastry from the oven. Push down the central circle of each pastry round to create a mini tart case with a raised pastry edge. Heap the chopped plums in the centre of each one, then scatter over the toasted almonds and cinnamon. Pop the tarts back in the oven for 5 minutes to warm them through and then serve.

Glistening, crispy filo pastry parcels allow the juices from baked banana and orange to collect into pools of fragrant deliciousness. Serve these desserts hot with cream.

Banana & Orange Filo Parcels

MAKES 4

2 bananas, about 325g (11oz) total weight
175g (6oz) drained canned mandarins
5 sheets of ready-made filo pastry, about 100g (3½oz) total weight
50g (2oz) salted butter, melted

Preheat the oven to 200°C/180°C fan/400°F/Gas Mark 6. Cut 4 pieces of foil roughly 15cm (6 inches) square.

Peel the bananas and cut into medium slices. Chop the mandarins roughly and set aside.

Lay your stack of filo pastry sheets lengthways and cut it in half vertically and horizontally to create 4 rectangular piles. Leave them under a clean tea towel to prevent the pastry drying out.

Take your first pile of filo pastry rectangles and brush each sheet with melted butter. Place one-quarter of the banana slices and chopped mandarins in the centre. Scrunch the edges of the pastry and bring them together to create a sack shape.

Place your parcel in the centre of a foil square, then scrunch the edges of the foil together to support the pastry, taking care to leave an opening at the top. Place the finished parcel on a baking sheet. Repeat the process for the remaining 3 piles of filo pastry.

Brush any remaining butter across the visible surfaces of the pastry parcels. Bake for 20 minutes, then remove the baking sheet from the oven and push all the foil flat. Place the parcels back in the oven for a further 15 minutes until they are golden brown all over. Serve immediately.

A sweet meringue tops a tangy and creamy pineapple filling in this fresh take on the classic lemon meringue pie.

Pineapple Meringue

SERVES 6–8

butter, for greasing
plain flour, for dusting
275g (9oz) ready-made
    unsweetened shortcrust pastry
    or 1 quantity of Low-carb Dessert
    Pastry (see page 170)
1 egg white, beaten
3 eggs
125g (4oz) drained canned
    pineapple chunks, finely chopped
175ml (6fl oz) pineapple juice
40g (1½oz) cornflour
125ml (4fl oz) mascarpone cheese
pinch of salt
1 tablespoon stevia powder (see
    page 187)
1 tablespoon raw organic local
    honey

Preheat the oven to 180°C/160°C fan/400°F/Gas Mark 4. Lightly grease a 20cm (8-inch) tart tin with a little butter.

Roll out the pastry on a worktop well dusted with flour to a thickness of about 3mm (⅛ inch). Roughly cut out a round slightly larger than the tin. Press the pastry into the tin and trim the excess with a sharp knife. Chill in the refrigerator for 20 minutes. Place a sheet of baking paper over the top of the tart case, then fill with dried beans or baking beans. Bake for 15–20 minutes and then remove from the oven and lift the paper and beans out – the pastry should feel dry and sandy to the touch. Brush with the beaten egg white and return to the oven for 5 minutes, until dry and golden.

While the tart base is baking, separate the eggs and place the yolks in a small bowl and the whites in a large bowl. Set aside.

Remove the tart base from the oven and set aside. Scatter the pineapple chunks over a baking tray and roast in the oven for 15 minutes to dry them out.

Stir the pineapple juice and cornflour together in a small saucepan. Bring to the boil, whisking continuously. When you have a thick, translucent paste, remove the pan from the heat and whisk in the mascarpone and egg yolks, followed by the roasted pineapple chunks.

Pour in the mascarpone mixture into the pastry base and smooth it out.

Now make the meringue. Place the bowl with the egg whites on a large saucepan of simmering water, making sure the bowl does not touch the water. Using an electric whisk, whisk the egg whites with the salt, stevia powder and honey until you have a dense white foam.

Gently spread the meringue across the top of the mascarpone mixture. To finish the top, use a mini blow torch or place under a preheated hot grill for 1–2 minutes until the meringue has some colour, if liked.

This fresh, breezy dessert is quick to make and is a sensationally sweet way to end a meal. Even better, it can be made a few hours in advance, but should be eaten on the day it is made.

Raspberry & Mint Sundae

SERVES 4

250ml (8fl oz) soured cream
140g (4½oz) fresh raspberries
140g (4½oz) red seedless grapes
2 teaspoons finely shredded mint

Line up your serving glasses and spoon out half the soured cream evenly between them.

Reserve 4 raspberries as decoration, then lightly mash the rest and spread them across the soured cream in the glasses. Chop each grape into quarters and distribute the pieces over the mashed raspberries. Add a sprinkling of mint to each glass, leaving a little for decoration.

Finish by spooning out the remaining soured cream. Pop a raspberry on the top of each dessert, followed by the remaining mint. Chill in the refrigerator until ready to serve.

Coconut water is the naturally sweet juice that comes from young tender, coconuts and it contains a unique mixture of nutrients. It's wonderful here, mixed with juicy peaches and crème fraîche.

Peach Fruit Fool

SERVES 4

250ml (8fl oz) coconut water
40g (1½oz) cornflour
250ml (8fl oz) crème fraîche
5 ripe peaches

Whisk the coconut water and cornflour together in a saucepan until smooth, then bring to the boil, whisking continuously. When the mixture has become translucent and thick, take it off the heat and leave it to cool completely, stirring occasionally. It will thicken more as it cools. Stir in the crème fraîche until well combined.

Cut 4 of the peaches in half and remove the stones. Dice the flesh into pieces not more than 1cm (½-inch) square. Place them in a large bowl and spoon over the crème fraîche mixture. Stir everything together, and then chill in the refrigerator for an hour.

Just before serving, spoon the fool into serving bowls. Cut the remaining peach in half and remove the stone, then slice up and use to decorate the fools.

The delicate flavour of fresh figs takes centre stage in this elegant dessert. The subtle creaminess makes the perfect finish to a spicy main course.

Fresh Fig Panna Cotta

SERVES 4

For the panna cotta
2–3 leaves of gelatine
250ml (8fl oz) milk
250ml (8fl oz) single cream
2 teaspoons white wine (optional)
½ teaspoon stevia powder (see
    page 187)

For the sauce
4 fresh figs, about 300g (10oz), plus
    1 extra for decorating
4 red seedless grapes, plus 4 extra
    for decorating

Place the leaves of gelatine in a bowl and cover with cold water (use 3 leaves of gelatine if you prefer a firmer set). Leave to soak for 5 minutes so that they become really floppy.

Meanwhile, heat the milk and cream together in a saucepan until hot but not boiling.

Remove the pan from the heat and stir in the softened gelatine, wine (if using) and stevia powder. Pour the mixture into 4 dariole moulds. Chill in the refrigerator for about 4 hours until set.

When you are ready to serve, make the sauce. Cut the figs in half, scoop out the flesh with a spoon and place it in a blender with the grapes (for a smoother sauce, peel the grapes first). Blend briefly until there are no large lumps remaining.

Briefly dip each dariole mould into a bowl of hand-hot water to loosen the panna cotta, making sure that no water comes over the top of the mould. Place an upturned serving plate over the top of the mould, then flip both over together, giving one or two sharp shakes as you do so. The panna cotta should slide neatly out of its mould on to the plate.

Distribute the fig purée between the plates of panna cotta. To decorate, slice the extra fig and the grapes very thinly and arrange across each dessert. Serve immediately.

Don't be fooled by the simplicity of the ingredients of this fruit salad because the taste is anything but. A combination of sweet, sour and perfume, it makes a wonderful conclusion to a rich or spicy meal. This salad works best with the delicate taste and low acidity of pink grapefruit..

Fragrant Fruit Salad

SERVES 4–6

2 ripe papayas
2 pink grapefruit
350g (11½oz) fresh lychees
 or 2 x 200g (7oz) cans lychees
 in juice
4 passion fruit

To prepare the papayas, cut them in half and scoop out the seeds with a spoon, then remove the skin with a vegetable peeler. Slice the flesh into roughly 1.5cm (¾-inch) square pieces. Place all the pieces in a large serving bowl.

Working over the bowl to catch the juice, prepare the grapefruit by cutting the rind and white pith off with a paring knife, then slicing either side of each segment to free them from the skin. Cut each segment in half and then add them to the bowl.

Peel the fresh lychees and remove the stones, or drain the cans of lychees. Chop the lychees up roughly.

Finally, cut the passion fruit in half and scoop out the seeds and pulp into the bowl. Stir gently to combine.

Leave the salad to sit for at least 30 minutes before serving to allow the flavours to mingle. This salad is best served at room temperature.

Ice Creams

Making a successful ice cream is more science than art, but these recipes give wonderfully soft and oh-so-smooth results that will leave everyone begging for more.

Chocolate Chip Ice Cream

MAKES ABOUT 1 LITRE (1¾ PINTS)

For the basic custard base
1 tablespoon agar powder (see page 186)
375ml (13fl oz) rice milk
2 egg yolks
375ml (13fl oz) double cream
15g (½oz) raw lucuma powder (see page 186)
4 teaspoons raw organic local honey

For the chocolate flavouring
25g (1oz) cocoa powder
2 teaspoons unsweetened vanilla extract
2 teaspoons stevia powder (see page 187)
50g (2oz) no-added-sugar milk chocolate, chopped into small pieces

To make the basic custard base, stir the agar powder into the rice milk in a saucepan. Bring to the boil and cook until the agar powder has dissolved – about 5 minutes.

Beat the egg yolks with the cream, lucuma powder and honey in a large bowl, then stir the hot rice milk into the mixture. Pour everything back into the pan and gently bring to the boil, stirring continuously so that the eggs don't curdle. When you begin to see bubbles rising to the surface, remove the pan from the heat.

Stir in the cocoa powder, vanilla extract and stevia powder. Leave the mixture to cool completely, giving it a stir from time to time. When it is cold, stir in the chocolate pieces.

Pour the cooled mixture into your ice cream maker and churn according to the manufacturer's instructions. If you don't have an ice cream maker, freeze the mixture in the bowl, then over the course of 2 hours, bring it out of the freezer every 30 minutes and blend it well in a food processor each time.

Transfer the ice cream to a 1-litre (1¾-pint) strong plastic tub with a lid, store in the freezer and use within a week.

Vanilla Ice Cream

MAKES ABOUT 1 LITRE (1¾ PINTS)

1 quantity of basic custard base, as above

For the vanilla flavouring
5 teaspoons unsweetened vanilla extract
¼ teaspoon salt

To make the custard base, follow the first two steps as in the recipe above.

Stir in the vanilla extract and salt. Leave the mixture to cool completely. It will set as it cools, but don't worry – just give it a stir from time to time.

Follow the last two steps as in the recipe above.

Roasted bananas are the basis of this easy ice cream, giving a delicious sweetness that is offset perfectly by the salty chunks of peanut. For best results, leave the ice cream to defrost for 15 minutes before serving.

Banana & Salted Peanut Ice Cream

MAKES ABOUT 1 LITRE (1¾ PINTS)

6 bananas, about 800g (1lb 9oz) total weight
75g (3oz) unsweetened crunchy peanut butter
125ml (4fl oz) double cream
75g (3oz) salted peanuts, finely chopped

Preheat the oven to 200°C/180°C fan/400°F/Gas Mark 6. Place the bananas in their skins in a roasting dish and bake for 20 minutes until blackened and soft.

Scrape out the banana flesh and juice into a bowl. Add the peanut butter and cream, and blend with a stick blender for a few seconds until smooth. Leave to cool.

Transfer the mixture to an ice cream maker and churn according to the manufacturer's instructions. If you don't have an ice cream maker, freeze the mixture in the bowl, then over the course of 2 hours, bring it out of the freezer every 30 minutes and blend it well in a food processor each time.

Stir in the peanuts, then transfer the ice cream to a 1-litre (1¾-pint) strong plastic tub with a lid, store in the freezer and use within a week.

This ice cream gives a triple whammy of sensual delight: first you're seduced by the gorgeous pinky orange colour, then just as you're tasting the creamy subtlety of the sweet papaya, you get the acid hit from the lime – terrific.

Papaya & Lime Ice Cream

MAKES ABOUT 750ML (1¼ PINTS)

grated rind of 2 unwaxed limes
125ml (4fl oz) fresh lime juice
2 tablespoons stevia powder (see page 187)
2 tablespoons agar powder (see page 186)
310ml (10½fl oz) double cream
2 ripe papayas, about 700g (1lb 7oz) total weight

Place the grated lime rind and juice, stevia powder and agar powder in a saucepan and heat gently until the stevia and agar have almost dissolved. Pour in the cream and bring to the boil, then remove the pan from the heat.

Cut the papayas in half and scoop out the seeds with a spoon, then remove the skin with a vegetable peeler. Place the flesh in a blender and blend until smooth. Stir the papaya purée into the hot cream. Leave the mixture to cool completely.

Pour the cooled mixture into an ice cream maker and churn according to the manufacturer's instructions. If you don't have an ice cream maker, freeze the mixture in the bowl, then over the course of 2 hours, bring it out of the freezer every 30 minutes and blend it well in a food processor each time.

Transfer the ice cream to a 750ml (1¼-pint) strong plastic tub with a lid and store in the freezer. Try to eat the ice cream as soon as possible, as it will gradually become more and more icy. For best results, leave the ice cream to defrost for about 15 minutes before serving.

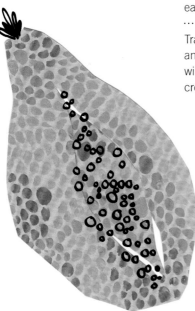

For a change from ice cream, this is a totally refreshing and summery frozen dessert, which is prepared as a solid block and then cut into slices to serve. For best results, use gorgeously ripe, juicy strawberries and eat within a couple of days of making it.

Strawberry Parfait

SERVES 8

sunflower oil, for oiling

700g (1lb 7oz) fresh strawberries

2 tablespoons agar powder (see page 186)

500ml (17fl oz) double cream

½ teaspoon ground black pepper

1–2 teaspoons stevia powder (see page 187) or raw organic local honey (optional)

Line a 22 x 11 x 7cm (8¾ x 4½ x 3-inch)/1kg (2lb) loaf tin with clingfilm and then smear the clingfilm with a thin layer of sunflower oil.

Hull the strawberries, then cut 100g (3½oz) of them into thin slices about 3mm (⅛inch) thick. Line the tin with the strawberries slices – they should stick to the clingfilm on the base and sides by themselves.

Stir the agar powder into the cream in a bowl until you can't see any powder left. Place the cream mixture with the remaining strawberries and the pepper in a blender or food processor and blend together. If your strawberries weren't very sweet, you could add the stevia powder or raw honey at this point to boost the flavour.

Pour the mixture into the loaf tin and freeze it for at least 4 hours. To serve, leave to defrost for 30 minutes. Turn the loaf tin upside down on to a serving plate and remove the tin to reveal your parfait, then peel off the clingfilm. Cut into slices with a large sharp knife.

Kulfi is an Indian ice cream commonly made with condensed milk, almonds and cardamom. I've used naturally sweet evaporated milk and pistachios instead. The nuttiness lends an irresistible texture. Though I've specified dariole moulds, small plastic drinking glasses are a good alternative.

Pistachio Kulfi

SERVES 6

75g (3oz) shelled unsalted pistachio nuts
4 tablespoons water
375ml (13fl oz) evaporated milk
125ml (4fl oz) whipping cream
1½ tablespoons stevia powder (see page 187)

Soak the pistachios in the measurement water for at least 4 hours or overnight.

Place the soaked nuts and any remaining water in a blender or food processor and add all the other ingredients. Blend for about 1 minute until the mixture has become a bit frothy and the texture is nearly smooth.

Line up 6 dariole moulds and half-fill each one. Use a tablespoon to scoop out the rubbly nut mixture that will have collected at the bottom of the blender and distribute it evenly between the moulds. Freeze for at least 4 hours until hardened.

To serve, sit the dariole moulds in a flat-based bowl. Pour warm water into the bowl until it reaches just below the rim. After about 5 seconds, remove the moulds and run a butter knife around the inside of each one. Turn the kulfi out on to serving plates. The chopped nut mixture will have coloured the outside of the kulfi, giving an attractive, green and purple-speckled effect. Leave to soften for 5–10 minutes before serving.

At one point in my life I lived in Paris and fell in love with a lychee yogurt from my local store to the point of obsession. I have done my best to reincarnate it here, minus any added sugar, which thanks to the inherent sweetness of lychees isn't necessary anyway. This frozen yogurt is quick to make and best enjoyed semifreddo, as a dreamy mouthful of cool perfection.

Lychee Frozen Yogurt

MAKES ABOUT 750ML (1¼ PINTS)

400g (13oz) pitted fresh or drained
    canned lychees
250ml (8fl oz) full-fat Greek yogurt
pinch of salt

Place half the lychees in a food processor and process until smooth. Transfer to a bowl and stir in the yogurt and salt.

Finely dice the remaining lychees, add to the bowl and stir together.

Ideally, you should now cover and leave the mixture in the refrigerator for an hour to allow the sweetness and flavours to develop, but if you're short of time, just skip this step.

Pour the mixture into a 750ml (1¼-pint) strong plastic tub with a lid and freeze for 45 minutes. Use an electric whisk to blend everything thoroughly, then freeze for a further 30 minutes. Whisk again. The frozen yogurt should now have the consistency of whipped cream and is ready to serve. Alternatively, keep it in the freezer until needed and leave it to defrost for 20 minutes, then whisk it with an electric whisk just before serving. The frozen yogurt will keep for up to a week.

Ginger is combined with the delicate flavour of melon in this refreshing, snowy-textured granita. Try it as a dessert in a decorative glass, topped with raspberries and balls of fresh melon.

Ginger Granita

**MAKES ABOUT 1 LITRE
(1¾ PINTS)**

2 Galia melons, about 2kg (4lb)
  in total
6 teaspoons fresh lemon juice
½ teaspoon ground ginger

Quarter the melons and scrape out all the seeds. Use a tablespoon to scrape all the flesh out and place it in a blender with the lemon juice and ginger. Blend until just smooth.

Pour the mixture into a 1-litre (1¾-pint) strong plastic tub with a lid. Freeze for 2 hours, giving a quick stir every 30 minutes or so. After this time, blend everything again in the blender. You'll now have a much paler mixture with an even consistency.

Return to the tub and freeze for a further 2 hours before serving. The granita needs to be consumed a couple of days after it is made or the texture will become too icy and hard.

The rum in this simple, dairy-free frozen dessert adds a bit of a kick and also helps keep the texture smooth. It's a great way to end a meal on a relaxed summer's day and I love its retro-kitsch vibe, especially when it's served with a cocktail umbrella and a slice of pineapple!

Piña Colada Ice

MAKES ABOUT 1.2 LITRES (2 PINTS)

2 x 425g (14oz) cans pineapple chunks in juice
310ml (10½fl oz) coconut cream (the liquid kind)
4 tablespoons white rum

Place all the ingredients in a food processor and process until well blended, then pour into a 1.5-litre (2½-pint) strong plastic tub with a lid.

Freeze for 3 hours, then blend in the food processor again briefly. Return to the tub and refreeze for about 30 minutes or until needed. This is best eaten within 48 hours or the texture will become too hard.

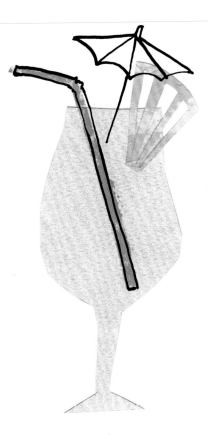

The smooth, intensely cold texture of real sorbet is unbeatable on a hot day and this recipe also has a hint of pepperiness, which gives an interesting contrast. Keeping sorbets silky is especially tricky when going sugar free because the sugar plays such an important role, but after experimenting a bit, I found a winning combination.

Orange & Star Anise Sorbet

MAKES ABOUT 500ML (17FL OZ)

500ml (17fl oz) fresh orange juice with bits
1 tablespoon agar powder (see page 186)
1 tablespoon stevia powder (see page 187)
2 star anise
large pinch of ground black pepper
2 egg whites

Pour the juice into a large saucepan. Stir in the agar powder, stevia powder, star anise and black pepper and then simmer for 5 minutes or until the agar has dissolved. Transfer the liquid to a jug and discard the star anise.

Using an electric whisk, whisk the egg whites in a bowl until they form soft peaks. While continuing to whisk, very slowly pour in the hot juice in a thin stream, which will create a sort of cooked meringue. Don't worry if there seems to be liquid under the meringue. Chill the mixture in the refrigerator for an hour or so until completely cold.

Pour the chilled mixture into your ice cream maker and churn according to the manufacturer's instructions. You can then transfer the sorbet to a 750ml (1¼-pint) strong plastic tub with a lid and store in the freezer. It will become harder over time, so eat within a couple of days. Leave to soften for 5 minutes before serving.

Watermelon and evaporated milk is an amazingly tasty combination, while a touch of Campari adds an adults-only angle to these vibrant stripy ice lollies – they're a firm favourite at beach or barbecue parties. Ice lolly moulds vary quite a lot in their volume, but this should make enough for at least 6.

Campari & Watermelon Lollies

MAKES ABOUT 500ML (17FL OZ)

300g (10oz) peeled and deseeded watermelon
1 tablespoon Campari
185ml (6½fl oz) evaporated milk

Place the watermelon flesh in a blender or food processor and blend until smooth. Stir in the Campari.

To create the stripes, first pour the watermelon mixture into your ice lolly moulds to fill each by one-third. Freeze for an hour.

Now pour in evaporated milk to fill a further one-third of your moulds. Attach foil to the top of each mould with an elastic band, then insert a lolly stick through the foil into the evaporated milk layer. Freeze for a further 45 minutes–1 hour until reasonably firm.

Remove the foil and top up with watermelon mixture, leaving a space at the top of the mould to allow for the expansion of the ice. Pop the lollies back in the freezer. They will be fully hardened after about 3 hours. The lollies are best served within a week.

Everyday Snacks

I love the windmill shape of these pretty Danish pastries. Keeping the skin on the apples not only makes them healthier but also gives the twists a more colourful look.

Cream Cheese & Apple Twists

MAKES 8

plain flour, for dusting
250g (8oz) ready-made puff pastry
2 dessert apples, cored and chopped into small pieces, skin left on
3 teaspoons water
50g (2oz) cream cheese
1 egg, beaten

Preheat the oven to 200°C/180°C fan/400°F/Gas Mark 6. Sprinkle a little flour across a baking sheet.

Place the chopped apple in a small saucepan with the measurement water and heat gently for about 5 minutes until softened.

Roll out the pastry on a worktop well dusted with flour to a rectangle about 35 x 18cm (14 x 7 inches), and about 3mm (⅛ inch) thick. Cut into 8 pastry squares. On each square, make a cut from each corner towards the centre using a sharp knife, stopping about halfway in.

Spread the cream cheese across the centre of each square and then distribute the apple on top of each portion of cream cheese.

To make the twist shape, bring the left-hand side of each corner into the centre. Secure the tips in place by brushing with the beaten egg, pressing together and sticking a cocktail stick through the middle. Repeat for the other pastries. Brush a little beaten egg across all visible pastry surfaces.

Transfer to the floured baking sheet and bake for 20 minutes until golden. Remove the cocktail sticks. These pastries are best served warm.

These snack bars are ready in minutes and make a filling mid-morning pick-me-up that should prevent you diving into the biscuit tin. Figs, nuts and seeds give texture and taste – simple but totally moreish.

Peanut Snack Bars

MAKES 12

200g (7oz) soft dried figs
100g (3½oz) unsweetened crunchy
   peanut butter
40g (1½oz) sunflower seeds
40g (1½oz) pumpkin seeds
40g (1½oz) wholemeal plain flour
2 tablespoons sunflower oil
2 teaspoons water

Remove the tough stalky part at the top of each fig. Place the figs in a food processor, add all the other ingredients and pulse until you have a mixture with the texture of fine crumbs. Press the crumbs firmly together to form a dough.

Roll out the dough on a worktop to a thickness of about 1cm (½ inch) – a rectangle about 18 x 15cm (7 x 6 inches) is perfect. If there are cracks, press the dough more firmly. Cut into 12 slices. Store in the refrigerator and eat within 7 days.

These bars are made from dense German-style rye bread – the kind that usually comes in a square block, pre-sliced. Rye bread is already packed full of nutrients and here I've added prunes, pumpkin seeds and dark chocolate to create a pleasingly portable snack for people on the go.

Chocolate & Rye Energy Bars

MAKES 8

sunflower oil, for oiling
4 tablespoons milk
1 egg
250g (8oz) German-style rye bread
100g (3½oz) pitted prunes
100g (3½oz) no-added-sugar plain dark chocolate
40g (1½oz) pumpkin seeds

Preheat the oven to 180°C/160°C fan/350°F/Gas Mark 4. Lightly oil a 22 x 11 x 7cm (8¾ x 4½ x 3-inch)/1kg (2lb) loaf tin with a little sunflower oil.

Whisk the milk and egg together in a large bowl. Crumble in the rye bread in smallish pieces. Give the mixture a stir, then leave to sit for about 10 minutes.

Finely chop the prunes and half the chocolate, then stir both into the rye mixture along with the pumpkin seeds.

Break the remaining chocolate into small pieces. Place in a heatproof bowl set over a saucepan of barely simmering water (make sure the base of the bowl doesn't touch the water), or in the microwave on a medium setting for about 45 seconds (my preferred method), until nearly all the chocolate has melted. Give it a stir and leave to rest for a couple of minutes until it has all melted. Stir the melted chocolate into the rye mixture.

Transfer the mixture to the loaf tin and smooth the top with a spatula. Bake for 20 minutes.

Leave to cool, then cut into slices. The bars will keep for up to a week in the refrigerator.

This is a fabulous, fudgy gingerbread made only with raw ingredients, so as well as being rammed full of goodness it takes just moments to make. It'll keep for up to 3 days in the refrigerator.

Raw Gingerbread

MAKES 12 PIECES

185g (6½oz) pitted dried dates
75g (3oz) raw cashew nuts
100g (3½oz) carrot, peeled and
　finely grated
75g (3oz) wholemeal plain flour
grated rind of 1 unwaxed orange
1 tablespoon sunflower oil
1 teaspoon ground ginger
1 teaspoon ground cinnamon
2 tablespoons flaked almonds

Place all the ingredients except the flaked almonds in a food processor and process for a minute or so until everything comes together in a doughy lump. Stir in the flaked almonds.

Use a spatula to scrape everything out and then pat the mixture into a square about 2.5cm (1 inch) thick. Cut into 12 pieces and transfer to a plastic tub with a lid. Chill in the refrigerator for 4 hours, or overnight, until the gingerbread has firmed to the texture of fudge.

Variation

You can make a gluten-free version of the gingerbread by replacing the wholemeal flour with a gluten-free flour blend.

This banana bread makes a nutritious snack: it's packed with bananas, which are rich in manganese and potassium, and the wholemeal flour and sunflower seeds contribute extra goodness in the form of fibre and Vitamins B and E. It's great just as it is, or with butter or even a slice of cheese.

Banana Bread

MAKES ABOUT 12 SLICES

4 ripe bananas, about 700g (1lb 7oz)
75g (3oz) unsalted butter, melted, plus extra for greasing
1 egg, beaten
150g (5oz) white plain flour
50g (2oz) wholemeal plain flour
4 teaspoons baking powder
½ teaspoon salt
75g (3oz) sunflower seeds

Preheat the oven to 200°C/180°C fan/400°F/Gas Mark 6. Lightly grease a 22 x 11 x 7cm (8¾ x 4½ x 3-inch)/1kg (2lb) loaf tin with a little butter.

Peel and mash the bananas in a large bowl (a few lumps are OK). Add the melted butter, followed by the egg, and stir well.

Add both flours, the baking powder and salt to the bowl. Gently fold everything together until well mixed. Set aside about 1 tablespoon of the sunflower seeds, then fold the rest into the mixture.

Use a spatula to transfer the mixture to the loaf tin. Shake gently to distribute it evenly in the tin and then smooth the top with the spatula. Sprinkle the reserved sunflower seeds on top.

Bake for 55–65 minutes until well browned and risen. Leave to cool in the tin.

Variation

You can make the banana bread dairy free by using dairy-free margarine in place of the butter. Make it vegan as well by omitting the egg and adding 4 tablespoons soya milk instead.

These waffles make a great choice to start your day – eaten with berries, they are a source of all the major food groups. I love them like this, with their hint of fragrant cardamom and a little sweetness from the rice milk.

Cardamom Waffles with Berries

SERVES 4

50g (2oz) unsalted butter, melted, plus extra for greasing
150g (5oz) wholemeal plain flour
150g (5oz) white plain flour
1 teaspoon baking powder
4 eggs, beaten
400ml (14fl oz) rice milk

1 green cardamom pod
150g (5oz) fresh blueberries
150g (5oz) fresh strawberries, hulled and halved
140g (4½oz) fresh raspberries

Pour the melted butter into a bowl and stir in both flours, the baking powder, eggs and half the rice milk to form a smooth paste. Gradually beat in the remaining rice milk.

Break open the cardamom pod and remove the seeds. Crush them with the back of a teaspoon, then sprinkle them into the batter by rubbing them between your fingers and thumb so that they crumble to dust. Stir in.

Preheat your waffle iron to medium-high and lightly grease with a little butter. Pour in the first portion of batter and cook for 4–5 minutes until the waffle is browned and crispy. Repeat the process until the batter is used up. If necessary, the cooked waffles can be kept warm in a low oven while the others are cooking.

Serve the waffles warm, scattered with the fresh berries.

These buns make the perfect project for a happy afternoon in the kitchen, mooching about and not doing anything too strenuous. The cinnamon-laced scent as the buns cook is totally uplifting too.

Swedish Cherry Buns

MAKES 12

For the dough
1 dessert apple, about 150g (5oz)
1 green cardamom pod
300g (10oz) strong white flour, plus extra for dusting
75g (3oz) wholemeal plain flour
7g (¼oz) sachet fast-action dried yeast
200ml (7fl oz) milk, plus a little extra if needed
1 egg
½ teaspoon salt

For the filling
25g (1oz) unsalted butter, very soft
2 teaspoons ground cinnamon
50g (2oz) soft dried apricots
50g (2oz) dried cherries

For the topping
2 tablespoons milk
20g (¾oz) shelled unsalted pistachio nuts, finely chopped

To make the dough, cut the apple in half and set one half aside, cut side down, for the filling. Core and roughly grate the other half (leave the skin on), then place in a large bowl. Break open the cardamom pod and remove the seeds. Crush them to a powder using the back of a teaspoon and add to the bowl with all the remaining dough ingredients. Stir well, then knead the mixture to bring it together into a dough – add a little more milk or flour, if necessary.

Knead the dough by hand on a worktop lightly dusted with flour for a further 5 minutes or using a freestanding electric mixer fitted with the dough hook.

Roll out the dough on the floured worktop to a 26cm (10¼-inch) square, about 5mm (¼ inch) thick.

Now make the filling. Beat the butter and cinnamon together and spread across the dough, taking care to make an even layer that reaches every edge. Core and roughly grate the reserved apple half (again, leave the skin on), and chop the apricots very finely, then stir them both together with the cherries. Distribute the mixture on top of the butter.

Roll the dough into a cylinder shape and cut into 12 slices. Place each slice facing upwards in a paper muffin case. Leave the muffin tin somewhere warm for 1–2 hours until the dough has at least doubled in size and filled the paper cases.

Preheat the oven to 220°C/200°C fan/425°F/Gas Mark 7. Brush each bun with a little of the milk and sprinkle with the pistachios. Bake for 12–15 minutes until the buns are golden. Serve warm or cold, they will keep surprisingly well for a couple of days (warm them before serving).

This is a seriously versatile loaf – serve it warm from the oven as a fragrant and welcoming treat when friends come round, eat it toasted and buttered for breakfast or just enjoy it with a slice of cheese as a nutritious snack.

Fruit Plait

MAKES ABOUT 15 SLICES

275g (9oz) strong white flour, plus extra for dusting
75g (3oz) wholemeal plain flour
2 teaspoons fast-action dried yeast
1½ teaspoons ground mixed spice
pinch of salt
1 large unwaxed orange, about 250g (8oz)
1 teaspoon sunflower oil, plus extra for oiling
40g (1½oz) sultanas
20g (¾oz) sunflower seeds
1 tablespoon milk

Lightly oil a baking sheet with a little sunflower oil.

Place the both flours in a bowl with the yeast, mixed spice and salt. Grate in the rind of the orange and then give everything a stir.

Juice the orange and scrape out all the nice juicy bits (avoiding the bitter white pith) into a measuring jug and make up to 250ml (8fl oz) with warm water.

Pour the liquid into the flour mixture and add the oil. Stir together as far as possible, then get your hands in and knead the mixture to a lovely soft and aromatic dough.

Knead the dough for 3–4 minutes on a worktop well dusted with flour. It should be really soft but not sticky – add a little extra flour if necessary. Knead in the sultanas and sunflower seeds.

Cut the dough into 3 equal-sized pieces. Roll each one into a sausage shape about 36cm (14 inches) long, tapered at both ends.

Plait the 3 sausage shapes together and pinch the ends to a point. Place the loaf on the baking sheet, then brush the milk across the top of the plait. Leave for 1–2 hours in a warm place until doubled in size.

Preheat the oven to 220°C/200°C fan/425°F/Gas Mark 7. Bake the loaf for 20 minutes until golden brown. Enjoy hot or cold.

Variation

For a vegan/dairy-free version of this recipe, use soya milk in place of the cows' milk.

In this porridge, the oats are left to soak in order for them to soften and for the flavours to mingle. Don't be put off by the extra time involved because making it is easily slotted into a morning routine – I like to do the preparation, go off and have a shower and then heat it and eat it. So simple!

Apple Porridge

SERVES 2

50g (2oz) rolled oats
310ml (10½fl oz) water
1 large dessert apple, about 200g (7oz), cored and roughly grated (leave the skin on)
2 tablespoons natural yogurt
1 tablespoon flaked Brazil nuts

Mix the oats, measurement water and grated apple together in a saucepan. Leave to soak for about 10 minutes, then simmer the mixture for 4–5 minutes until thickened and slightly translucent.

Spoon out the porridge into 2 bowls. Add a tablespoonful of yogurt to the top of each, then sprinkle the flaked Brazil nuts over the top and serve.

Variations

For a dairy-free breakfast, use soya yogurt. Use gluten-free oats for a gluten free version of this recipe.

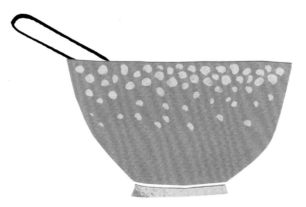

This is my perfect muesli – not too sweet, by turns crunchy and chewy, and with a great selection of nuts, seeds and fruit that means I can bask in the glow of racking up several of my 5-a-day by 8am. Try it with natural Greek yogurt or with fresh milk.

Mango & Cranberry Muesli

MAKES ABOUT 15 SERVINGS

125g (4oz) rye or wholewheat flakes
1 teaspoon sunflower oil
½ teaspoon ground cinnamon
40g (1½oz) pumpkin seeds
25g (1oz) flaked coconut
25g (1oz) flaked almonds
200g (7oz) rolled oats
50g (2oz) dried unsweetened
   mango, finely chopped
40g (1½oz) dried unsweetened
   cranberries
25g (1oz) shelled raw pistachio nuts

Preheat the oven to 180°C/160°C fan/350°F/Gas Mark 4. Get out 2 baking sheets. Spread your rye or wheat flakes out on 1 baking sheet.

Stir the oil and cinnamon together in a bowl. Tip in the pumpkin seeds, coconut and almonds and stir until evenly coated in the oil and cinnamon mixture. Spread the mixture on to the second baking sheet. Place both baking sheets in the oven. After 10 minutes, remove the nut mixture but leave the rye/wheat flakes for a further 5 minutes to get nicely crisp. Leave everything to cool completely.

Place the oats in a 1-litre (2-pint) clip-top jar. Add the mango, cranberries and pistachios. Finally, pour in the rye/wheat flakes and the toasted nut mixture. Give everything a stir and a shake and clip the lid shut. The muesli should keep well for a couple of weeks.

Variation

I've used unsweetened cranberries here, but they are a little tart. You can substitute them with raisins if you prefer a sweeter muesli.

These grissini cost a fraction of the artisanal ones from your local deli, but their delicate forms and sprinkling of poppy seeds mean they look and taste just as good. Try them dipped into hummus or a spicy salsa.

Poppy Seed Grissini

MAKES ABOUT 50

125ml (4fl oz) warm water
1 teaspoon fast-action dried yeast
1 teaspoon good-quality fresh apple juice
150g (5oz) strong white flour, plus extra for dusting
2 tablespoons wholemeal plain flour
¼ teaspoon fine salt
2 tablespoons olive oil, plus extra for oiling
1 teaspoon milk
1 tablespoon poppy seeds

Lightly oil a couple of baking sheets.

Stir together the measurement warm water, yeast and apple juice in a bowl.

Place both flours and salt in a large bowl. Pour in the yeast liquid and the oil, mix it in and bring together into a dough.

Knead for a good couple of minutes on a worktop well dusted with flour until you have a soft and supple dough – add a little extra flour if it seems too sticky.

Roll out the dough on the floured worktop to a rectangle about 20 x 25cm (8 x 10 inches), and about 5mm (¼ inch) thick. Brush the top with the milk and then scatter over the poppy seeds.

Using a ruler and a pizza cutter, cut the rectangle along the long sides into 25 strips about 1cm (½ inch) wide.

Pick up a strip and gently stretch it so that it is roughly double its length (though don't let the strip get too thin in any one spot or it will overcook later on). Break it in half and twist each half 2 or 3 times before placing it on the baking sheet. Repeat for the remaining strips.

Leave the strips to rise for about an hour in a warm place until they have roughly doubled in thickness.

Preheat the oven to 200°C/180°C fan/400°F/Gas Mark 6. Bake the grissini for 15 minutes, then reduce the oven temperature to 140°C/120°C fan/275°F/Gas Mark 1 for a further 5–10 minutes until they are golden brown and hard all the way through. Leave them to cool on a wire rack, then store them in a tall airtight jar.

Variation

Use soya milk in place of the milk if you want a dairy-free recipe.

These scones are a favourite snack of my niece Cecily – she loves the crunchy, cheesy crust and fluffy centre. They are lovely cold, but even better slightly warm from the oven and spread with butter or eaten just as they are.

Smoked Cheese & Apple Scones

MAKES 6

1 dessert apple, about 150g (5oz)
100g (3½oz) Bavarian smoked cheese
75g (3oz) wholemeal plain flour
75g (3oz) white plain flour, plus extra for dusting
2½ teaspoons baking powder
1 tablespoon sunflower oil, plus extra for oiling
1 egg, beaten
2 teaspoons milk
1 tablespoon sunflower seeds

Preheat the oven to 220°C/200°C fan/425°F/Gas Mark 7. Lightly oil a baking sheet with sunflower oil.

Grate each side of the apple in turn against a box grater until you reach the core, working round the apple until all the flesh has been grated, then discard the core. Place the grated apple in a bowl. Next, grate the cheese and add to the bowl, then add both flours, the baking powder and oil.

Add the egg and stir everything together to create a soft and somewhat sticky dough.

Dust a worktop lightly with flour and flatten the dough to a thickness of about 3cm (1¼ inches). Use a 6cm (2½-inch) round cookie cutter to cut out your scones, gathering together the trimmings as necessary, until you have used up all the dough – you should get 6, but it does depend on the exact thickness of the dough. Place them on the baking sheet and then brush them with the milk and scatter the sunflower seeds on top.

Bake the scones for 15 minutes until risen and browned. They will spread a little as they cook. Leave to cool on a wire rack.

Inspired by the good old chicken korma, this tasty blend of spicy cashews, almonds and pumpkin seeds mixed with flaked coconut and pieces of dried mango will liven up any hike.

Spiced Trail Mix

MAKES 425G (14OZ)

150g (5oz) raw cashew nuts
140g (4½oz) whole almonds
75g (3oz) pumpkin seeds
2 teaspoons sunflower oil
1 tablespoon garam masala
50g (2oz) dried unsweetened
  mango, finely chopped
25g (1oz) flaked coconut salt

Place the cashews, almonds and seeds in a large frying pan over a medium-high heat. Dry-fry for about 10 minutes, stirring occasionally, until the nuts have started to brown and the pumpkin seeds start to pop.

Remove the pan from the heat. Mix the oil and garam masala together, then add to the pan and quickly give everything a good stir. Add salt to taste and then leave everything to cool completely.

Place the mango in an airtight jar, add the coconut and cooled nut mixture and give the jar a shake – your spicy snack is ready to go.

Pumpkin seeds are fantastically nutritious, but can be uninspiring eaten raw. After a rapid roasting and a super-tasty umami coating, they turn into the queen of snacks.

Pumpkin Pops

MAKES 300G (10OZ)

1 teaspoon light soy sauce
2 teaspoons water
300g (10oz) pumpkin seeds

Preheat the oven to 200°C/180°C fan/400°F/Gas Mark 6.

Mix the soy sauce and measurement water together in a large bowl. Pour in the pumpkin seeds and stir until they are lightly coated in the soy mixture.

Spread the seeds out on a baking sheet and place it in the oven. After about 8 minutes you'll hear slight popping noises coming from the oven as the seeds expand. Remove them from the oven after 10–12 minutes, when the majority of the seeds will have swelled and the coating has dried.

Leave to cool completely, then store in an airtight jar and eat within a week.

For
Children

These cheese-flavoured, milk-enriched breadsticks taste great by themselves or dipped into a little hummus. The kids love making the supple dough, providing a fun activity for an afternoon as well as a snack.

Cheesy Breadsticks

MAKES 16

150g (5oz) strong white flour, plus extra for dusting
150g (5oz) wholemeal plain flour
2 teaspoons fast-action dried yeast
1 teaspoon olive oil, plus extra for oiling
1 teaspoon mustard
250ml (8fl oz) warm milk, plus extra for brushing
100g (3½oz) Cheddar cheese or other hard cheese, grated
40g (1½oz) brown linseeds

Lightly oil a couple of baking sheets with a little olive oil.

Place both flours, the yeast, oil and mustard in a bowl. Pour in the warm milk and knead the mixture until it comes together as a soft dough.

Knead in the cheese, then continue kneading on a worktop well dusted with flour for a minute, adding a little extra flour if it feels too sticky – the dough should be very soft, but shouldn't stick to your fingers.

Cut the dough into 16 equal-sized pieces, then roll and stretch each one to form a breadstick about 25cm (10 inches) long. Brush the tops of the breadsticks with some warm milk. Pour the linseeds on to a large plate and roll each breadstick in the seeds before placing them on the baking sheets.

Leave the breadsticks to rise for an hour in a warm place until roughly doubled in size.

Preheat the oven to 220°C/200°C fan/425°F/Gas Mark 7. Bake the breadsticks for 10 minutes. Leave to cool on a wire rack.

My children are always complaining that they are hungry, but it's hard to keep their hands out of the biscuit tin. If that sounds familiar, then try offering these tomato and herb spirals warm from the oven as a tempting alternative to sugary snacks.

Tomato & Herb Spirals

MAKES 8

For the dough
sunflower oil, for oiling
2 teaspoons fast-action dried yeast
250ml (8fl oz) hand-hot water
1 tablespoon tomato purée
300g (10oz) strong white flour, plus extra for dusting
75g (3oz) wholemeal plain flour
pinch of salt

For the filling
75g (3oz) cooked carrot
3 tablespoons tomato purée
3 tablespoons milk
½ teaspoon dried oregano
50g (2oz) Cheddar cheese or other hard cheese, grated

Lightly oil a 25 x 16cm (10 x 6¼-inch) baking dish with a little sunflower oil.

To make the dough, stir the yeast, measurement hand-hot water and tomato purée together in a jug. Place both flours in a bowl with the salt. Stir in the liquid, then knead the mixture to bring it together into a dough.

Knead by hand on a worktop lightly dusted with flour for a further couple of minutes or using a freestanding electric mixer fitted with the dough hook.

Roll out the dough on the floured worktop into a 26cm (10¼-inch) square, about 5mm (¼ inch) thick.

Now make the filling. Place the cooked carrot, tomato purée, milk and oregano in a food processor or blender and process until smooth. Spread the mixture across the top of the dough.

Roll the dough into a cylinder and cut into 8 equal-sized slices. Place each slice facing upwards in the baking dish. Leave somewhere warm for 1–2 hours until the dough has more than doubled in size and the spirals have completely filled the dish. Sprinkle with the grated cheese.

Preheat the oven to 220°C/200°C fan/425°F/Gas Mark 7. Bake the spirals for 12–15 minutes until they are golden and all the dough is cooked. Serve warm or cold.

Dates and roasted butternut squash help to provide the all-important 'squidge' factor in these brownies and also offer a great way to give kids extra nutrients.

Chocolate Brownies

MAKES 16

sunflower oil, for oiling
200g (7oz) butternut squash
100g (3½oz) unsalted butter, chopped
2 teaspoons stevia powder (see page 187)
75g (3oz) no-added-sugar plain dark chocolate, broken into pieces
3 eggs
100g (3½oz) pitted dried dates
50g (2oz) wholemeal plain flour
50g (2oz) white plain flour
1 teaspoon baking powder
pinch of salt
50g (2oz) walnuts, chopped

Variation

Use dairy-free margarine in place of butter for a dairy-free version of this recipe.

Preheat the oven to 200°C/180°C fan/400°F/Gas Mark 6. Lightly oil a 20cm (8-inch) square baking tin with sunflower oil, or line the tin with baking parchment.

Deseed the butternut squash and chop into pieces about 2.5cm (1 inch) square. You can keep the skin on – it provides extra nutrients and you'll never notice it in the finished brownies. Spread the chopped squash out in the baking tin and roast for 20 minutes until soft. Leave to cool for about 10 minutes.

Meanwhile, place the butter, stevia powder and chocolate in a saucepan over a low heat, stirring occasionally. As soon as most of it has melted, remove the pan from the heat. Leave to stand until everything has melted.

Place the roasted squash, eggs and dates in a food processor and process for about 1 minute until the mixture is as smooth as possible. Now add both flours, the baking powder and salt, followed by the melted chocolate mixture. Process for about 30 seconds until everything is really well combined. Stir in the walnuts.

Spread the mixture across the baking tin and smooth it flat with a spatula. Bake for 12–15 minutes until the brownie has shrunk away from the sides of the tin but is still squidgy in the middle. Leave to cool in the tin, then cut into 16 pieces.

This recipe uses basic science to fascinating effect – colour-changing pancakes, packed with goodness, all thanks to grated beetroot and a few common ingredients. It's the perfect treat for budding chemists everywhere. Watch how the lusciously pink batter darkens or lightens, then see more magic happen in the pan. If only all cookery was so dramatic!

Magic Pancakes

SERVES 4

150g (5oz) plain flour
50g (2oz) wholemeal plain flour
1 egg
125ml (4fl oz) milk
2 tablespoons sunflower oil, plus extra for frying
75g (3oz) finely grated fresh beetroot
4 tablespoons soured cream, plus extra (optional) to serve
1 teaspoon baking powder
1 teaspoon bicarbonate of soda
225g (7½oz) fresh blueberries
cooked bacon, to serve (optional)

Place both flours in a bowl. Stir in the egg, milk and oil until you have a smooth batter. Add the grated beetroot to create a lovely pink colour.

Now transfer half the batter to a different bowl. To the first bowl add the soured cream and baking powder. The batter will become marginally more pinky red.

To the second bowl add the bicarbonate of soda. After a few minutes, you'll notice the colour darken to a purply pink.

Divide the blueberries evenly between the 2 batters and stir them in.

Heat a large frying pan over a medium heat and smear with a little sunflower oil. Use a tablespoon to add dollops of batter to the pan – depending on the size of your pan, you might fit 3 or 4 dollops on at a time. You'll see bubbles popping on the surface. After 1–2 minutes, when the bubbles ease off and the pancakes lose their gloss, flip them over and fry for a further minute or so until browned.

The bicarbonate pancakes will change from purple to yellow, while the baking powder pancakes will still be a violent pink. Enjoy them warm, with extra soured cream and bacon if you like.

Variation

You could make this recipe dairy free by using soya milk and soya yogurt in place of the cows' milk and soured cream.

These simple raw flapjacks are made almost entirely of oats, nuts and fruit, yet they combine to create a moreish snack. The fact they are frozen makes them especially appealing to kids.

Apple Freezer Flapjacks

MAKES 10

sunflower oil, for oiling
150g (5oz) rolled oats
50g (2oz) unsweetened smooth cashew nut butter
40g (1½oz) seedless raisins
25g (1oz) unsalted butter
1 large dessert apple, about 200g (7oz)

Variation

Use gluten-free oats for a gluten free version of this recipe.

Lightly oil a 22 x 11 x 7cm (8¾ x 4½ x 3-inch)/1kg (2lb) loaf tin with a little sunflower oil.

....

Put the oats in a food processor and pulse 3 or 4 times until you have a textured powder. Add the cashew nut butter, raisins and butter, then continue pulsing until the mixture is even in texture and the raisins have been thoroughly chopped up. Remove roughly half the mixture and set aside.

....

Roughly grate each side of the apple in turn against a box grater until you reach the core, working round the apple until all the flesh has been grated, then discard the core. Add the grated apple to the food processor and blend it with the remaining oat mixture for 4–5 seconds until smooth. Stir in the reserved oat mixture.

....

Scoop the mixture into the loaf tin and smooth down the top with the back of a spoon. Use a sharp knife to cut the mixture into 10 pieces. Freeze for at least an hour in a strong plastic tub with a lid (they'll keep for up to a week like this), then defrost for 10 minutes before eating.

This quick and easy chocolate treat requires no cooking and offers a nutritious mixture of dried fruit, nuts and seeds, all encased in a buttery chocolate mass. I've used wholemeal crackers to give an element of biscuity texture, but if you want something with no added salt, use sugar-free baby rusks instead.

Chocolate Refrigerator Cake

MAKES 8 SLICES

sunflower oil, for greasing
100g (3½oz) no-added-sugar milk chocolate, broken into pieces
50g (2oz) unsalted butter, chopped
50g (2oz) dried apricots, finely chopped
50g (2oz) unsweetened wholemeal crackers, crushed
25g (1oz) desiccated coconut
25g (1oz) flaked almonds
2 tablespoons pumpkin seeds

Lightly oil a 22 x 11 x 7cm (8¾ x 4½ x 3-inch)/1kg (2lb) loaf tin with a little sunflower oil.

Place the chocolate and butter in a saucepan over a low heat, stirring occasionally. As soon as most of it has melted, remove the pan from the heat and leave to stand until everything has melted.

Stir all the other ingredients into the melted chocolate mixture until everything is thoroughly combined.

Transfer the mixture to the loaf tin and press it down firmly with the back of a metal tablespoon to compact it and flatten the surface. Chill in the refrigerator for 30 minutes.

Run a butter knife between the edge of the tin and the cake to extract it from the tin and then slice it into 8 pieces with a sharp knife. Store in an airtight container in the refrigerator for up to 3 days.

These sticky buns are made from the same kind of enriched dough as doughnuts but are baked rather than fried so they contain less fat – and little hands can help with the whole process. These are lovely eaten warm.

Sticky Doughnut Buns

MAKES 10

1 tablespoon sunflower oil, plus extra for oiling
85ml (3¼fl oz) warm milk
1 teaspoon fast-action dried yeast
1 teaspoon good-quality fresh apple juice
1 teaspoon stevia powder (see page 187)
225g (7½oz) strong white flour, plus extra for dusting
¼ teaspoon ground nutmeg
25g (1oz) unsalted butter, melted
1 egg, beaten
2 teaspoons raw organic local honey, warmed
½ teaspoon ground cinnamon

Lightly oil a baking sheet with a little sunflower oil.

Stir the milk and yeast together with the stevia powder and apple juice in a jug. Mix the flour and nutmeg together in a bowl. Pour in the milk mixture, then stir in the melted butter and egg. Knead the mixture to bring it together into a dough.

Knead by hand on a worktop lightly dusted with flour for a further couple of minutes or using a freestanding electric mixer fitted with the dough hook until you have a soft and supple dough. You may need a little extra flour – the dough shouldn't be sticky.

Divide the dough into 10 equal-sized pieces and roll each one into a ball. Space them out evenly on the baking sheet and cover with a damp tea towel. Leave somewhere warm for an hour or so until they have doubled in volume.

Preheat the oven to 200°C/180°C fan/400°F/Gas Mark 6. Brush the tops of the buns with the warmed honey and then bake for 12–15 minutes until they are a rich golden brown colour and sound hollow when tapped on the bottom.

Sprinkle the warm buns with the cinnamon and serve.

Variation

Add 40g (1½oz) raisins to the dough if you want a fruited bun

These soft cookie stars make a good low-sugar finger food for toddlers and don't contain any added salt. A little wholemeal flour (and raw lucuma powder if you have some – see page 186) adds fibre and nutrients.

Ginger Stars

MAKES ABOUT 20

100g (3½oz) white plain flour, plus extra for dusting
50g (2oz) wholemeal flour
75g (3oz) unsalted butter, chilled and cut into chunks, plus extra for greasing
1 tablespoon raw lucuma powder (see page 186, optional)
1½ teaspoons ground ginger
1 teaspoon baking powder
1 small ripe banana, about 110g (3¾oz), peeled and mashed
1 tablespoon milk
40g (1½oz) raisins

Preheat the oven to 200°C/180°C fan/400°F/Gas Mark 6. Lightly grease a couple of baking sheets with a little butter.

Mix both flours together in a bowl, add the butter and rub in with your fingertips until the mixture resembles breadcrumbs (you can pulse the ingredients in a food processor instead, if you prefer).

Stir in the lucuma powder, if using, ginger, baking powder and mashed banana. Knead everything together into a soft dough. If it seems sticky, add a little more flour.

Roll out the dough on a worktop dusted with flour to a thickness of 5mm (¼ inch). Use a 6cm (2½-inch) star cookie cutter to cut out star shapes, rerolling the trimmings as necessary, until you have used up all the dough. Place the stars on the baking sheets.

Brush the stars with the milk. Decorate with the raisins, pushing them firmly into position. Bake the stars for 10–12 minutes until they are risen, slightly browned and cooked all the way through. Leave them to cool on a wire rack.

Crunchy cornflake cakes are a perennial favourite with children, but instead of loading these with syrup I have used peanut butter as a base. This means they are not only far lower in sugar but also higher in nutrients – peanuts are a great source of protein and vitamin E.

Crispy Cakes

MAKES 12

40g (1½oz) unsalted butter, cut into chunks
125g (4oz) unsweetened crunchy peanut butter
3 tablespoons dried milk powder
1½ tablespoons cocoa powder
1 tablespoon raw organic local honey
50g (2oz) unsweetened cornflakes
50g (2oz) raisins

Line a 12-cup cupcake tin with paper cupcake cases.

Place the butter, peanut butter, milk powder, cocoa powder and honey in a saucepan over a low heat until the butter has melted. Stir until everything has combined.

Stir in the cornflakes and raisins.

Divide the cornflake mixture between the paper cupcake cases. Chill in the refrigerator for about 30 minutes until the crispy cakes have set. They are best eaten the same day.

These little semicircular parcels are made from a yeast dough, but what makes them unusual is the fact that they are fried, not baked. This is because this recipe is based on one from the Middle Ages where oven baking was a rarity. The benefits are not only speed and a lovely buttery crust but also that they can be easily cooked over an open fire – which made them an instant hit with my children!

Apple & Blackberry Parcels

MAKES 6 OR 8

For the dough
½ dessert apple, about 75g (3oz)
100g (3½oz) plain flour
100g (3½oz) wholemeal plain flour
7g (¼oz) sachet fast-action dried
    yeast
175ml (6fl oz) warm milk
pinch of salt
100g (3½oz) unsalted butter

For the filling
2½ dessert apples, about 375g
    (12oz) total weight
35g (1¼oz) whole hazelnuts,
    roughly chopped
70g (2½oz) fresh blackberries
½ teaspoon ground cinnamon

Core and roughly grate the apple half (leave the skin on), then place in a large bowl. Add both flours, the yeast, warm milk and salt and knead everything together into a soft dough (you may need to add a little extra flour if it feels sticky). Cover the bowl with a clean tea towel and leave somewhere warm for an hour or so until the dough has doubled in volume.

Meanwhile, for the filling, roughly grate each side of the apples in turn against a box grater until you reach the core, working round each apple until all the flesh has been grated. Discard the core. Mix the grated apple with the hazelnuts in a bowl, then stir in the blackberries and cinnamon.

Divide the dough into 6 or 8 equal-sized portions (depending on the size of your frying pan). Flatten each one into a round about 5mm (¼ inch) thick. Lightly moisten the outer edges with a drop of water. Place a dollop of filling on one side of each round and then fold the round in half, sealing it closed by pressing the edges together with a fork.

Heat a frying pan over a medium heat and add a generous amount of butter. Fry the parcels for about 3–5 minutes on each side until crispy and golden brown.

Variation

Omit the hazelnuts if you want a nut-free recipe. If you want a dairy-free or vegan recipe, use dairy-free margarine in place of butter and soya milk in place of cows' milk.

You can enjoy these fritters just as they are, or for a sweeter treat, drizzle a little maple syrup over the top just before serving. Although I've used pineapple, sliced banana works well too.

Pineapple Fritters

MAKES ABOUT 8

50g (2oz) white plain flour
2 tablespoons wholemeal plain flour
4 tablespoons milk
1 egg, beaten
430g (14oz) can pineapple rings in juice, drained and juice reserved
sunflower oil, for frying

Note

This recipe uses very hot oil, so don't allow children near the saucepan and don't leave it unattended at any time.

Mix both flours, the milk and egg with 2 tablespoons of the pineapple juice in a bowl until you have a batter with the consistency of Greek yogurt.

Pat the pineapple rings dry with kitchen paper.

Leave the batter to stand while you fill a heavy-based saucepan with sunflower oil to a depth of about 3mm (⅛ inch). Heat the oil to 160–170°C/325–340°F – if you don't have a cooking thermometer, it's about the right temperature when it will brown a small cube of bread in 18 seconds.

Have a plate with a few sheets of kitchen paper ready by the pan. Depending on the size of your pan, you can probably fry 1–2 pineapple rings at a time.

Using a fork, first dip a pineapple ring into the batter so that it is completely coated, then carefully lower it into the hot oil. After about 1 minute, the side in the oil will have become crisp and brown; use the fork to flip it over. Fry for a further 1 minute, then use the fork to lift it out and place it on the kitchen paper to drain. Leave the fritters to cool for a few minutes before eating because they will be very hot.

It's easy to create slushy ice treats in exciting flavours and colours – and with a proper deep freeze, you won't have to wait too long for them either. You can use the juices and ready-made smoothie I've mentioned here or choose your own, just make sure they are dairy free and don't contain added sugar.

Stripy Snow Cones

MAKES 4

375ml (13fl oz) pineapple juice
375ml (13fl oz) black grape juice
250ml (8fl oz) strawberry-based
    dairy-free smoothie
125ml (4fl oz) water

You'll need 3 x 700ml (1 pint 3fl oz) square or rectangular strong plastic tubs with lids. Pour the pineapple juice into one, the grape juice into the second and the strawberry smoothie mixed with the measurement water into the third. Place in the deep freeze for 1½ hours.

....

While the juice freezes, make your cones. Cut 4 circles from foil 25cm (10 inches) in diameter – draw round a dinner plate or something similar. Cut 2 circles the same size from decorative paper – I like to use wrapping paper, which can be themed if necessary. Cut the wrapping paper circles in half and set aside.

....

Fold each foil circle in half with the shiny side outermost. Now fold each half into thirds so that you end up with a triangular shape. If you look at the top of the triangle, you'll see that the layers of foil have created a series of triangular pockets. Push your fingers into one pocket and open it out to form a cone. Make sure you can see the matt side of the foil as you look inside the cone – this is vital to ensure you have created a watertight container. Stick a piece of adhesive tape on the seam of the cone to hold everything in place.

....

Fold each decorative paper semicircle into thirds to create an outer sleeve for each foil cone. Use adhesive tape to secure.

....

Once your juices and smoothie have had their allotted time in the freezer, bring them out and use a fork to mash into a granular, snowy texture. Lay the cones on their sides and spoon out an even amount of the pineapple ice into each one. Next, add a layer of grape ice. Finally, divide the strawberry smoothie ice between each cone. Serve the cones full of stripy ice immediately, with a straw and teaspoon poked into each one.

Treats &
Party Food

Cream, whisky and a sprinkling of edible gold stars and gold dust make these melt-in-the-mouth truffles extra special. Look for stars or other decorations made without added sugar.

Glittering Chocolate Truffles

MAKES ABOUT 15

100g (3½oz) no-added-sugar plain dark chocolate, broken into small pieces
25g (1oz) unsalted butter, chopped
4 tablespoons single cream
3 teaspoons whisky
15g (½oz) cocoa powder
1 teaspoon edible gold stars or edible gold dust

Place the chocolate and butter with the cream in a small saucepan over a low heat until they have melted, stirring occasionally. Stir in the whisky, then leave the mixture to cool. Place it in the refrigerator for about 1 hour until it hardens.

Sift the cocoa on to a plate and place a second plate alongside. Scoop out a heaped teaspoonful of the truffle mixture and quickly roll it into a ball in your palms. Place it on the plate with the cocoa and gently shake the plate from side to side until the truffle is well coated, then transfer the truffle to the clean plate. Repeat until all the truffle mixture is used up.

Sprinkle the edible gold stars or some edible gold dust over the truffles to give a touch of magic and sparkle. The truffles will keep in the refrigerator for up to a week.

I find fruity soft-centred chocolates irresistible, so these little hearts tick all the boxes for me. You'll need some small silicone chocolate moulds to make them, but these are easily available from cook shops or online.

Apricot Hearts

MAKES ABOUT 18

125g (4oz) no-added-sugar plain dark chocolate, broken into small pieces
25g (1oz) dried apricots
4 tablespoons water
25g (1oz) cream cheese
15g (½oz) ground almonds

Place 100g (3½oz) of the chocolate pieces in a heatproof bowl set over a saucepan of barely simmering water (make sure the base of the bowl doesn't touch the water), or in the microwave on a medium setting for about 45 seconds (my preferred method), until nearly all the chocolate has melted. Give it a stir and leave to rest for a couple of minutes until it has all melted.

Use a teaspoon to smear a layer of melted chocolate around the inside of each mould, making sure the sides and bases are well covered. Chill in the refrigerator for about 30 minutes until set.

Meanwhile, finely chop the apricots, place them in a small saucepan with the measurement water and heat them gently for 5 minutes. Pour the mixture into a mug and add the cream cheese. Insert a stick blender and blend to create a relatively smooth paste. Stir in the ground almonds. Spoon ½ teaspoonful of apricot filling into each chocolate and use the tip of your finger to smooth it in place so that none of the filling is protruding from the mould. Chill in the refrigerator for a further 30 minutes.

Finally, melt the remaining chocolate as before. Use a butter knife to spread an even layer of melted chocolate over the top of the apricot filling. Chill the chocolates for a further 30 minutes until set, then gently pull the silicone apart to release each heart. Turn them out on to a plate and keep chilled until ready to serve. They can be kept for a couple of days in the refrigerator.

Note

Be careful when melting the chocolate – it can be a rather temperamental beast, particularly in situations where you want an attractive finish. The key things to remember are not to let it get too hot and not to allow water into the melted chocolate, otherwise it will 'seize' and turn grainy and paste-like. If this happens, you will have to throw it out and start again.

Here I've combined wholemeal flour and no-added-sugar chocolate to create a healthier version of an enduring favourite – they are always the first to go at a party.

Mini Chocolate Eclairs

MAKES ABOUT 18

For the choux pastry
sunflower oil, for oiling
50g (2oz) unsalted butter
175ml (6fl oz) water
100g (3½oz) wholemeal plain flour
2 eggs, beaten

For the topping
100g (3½oz) no-added-sugar milk chocolate, broken into small pieces
2 tablespoons water

For the filling
250ml (8fl oz) whipping cream

Preheat the oven to 200°C/180°C fan/400°F/Gas Mark 6. Lightly oil 2 baking sheets, then run them under the cold tap in order to wet the surface. Tip the excess water away.

Heat the butter and measurement water in a saucepan until the mixture boils. Take the pan off the heat, add the flour and quickly whisk everything together (this requires quite a bit of arm strength, so you might want to use an electric whisk). Leave the mixture to cool for a minute, then whisk in the eggs until you have smooth paste with the consistency of thick custard.

Transfer the paste to a food bag. Snip off the corner, starting your cut about 1cm (½ inch) along the side of the bag. Pipe out sausage shapes of the paste about 7–8cm (3–3¼ inches) long on to the prepared baking sheets, making sure you space them well apart. It can be hard to finish the sausage shapes neatly, though a flick of the wrist usually works well. Use a moistened finger to gently smooth out any lumps that result.

Pop the baking sheets into the oven. After 10 minutes, increase the oven temperature to 220°C/200°C fan/425°F/Gas Mark 7 and bake the éclairs for a further 10 minutes until they are golden brown. Make a small hole in the side of each one with a skewer to release the steam, then leave them to cool on a wire rack.

Meanwhile, for the topping, place the chocolate and the measurement water in a small saucepan over a low heat until the chocolate has melted, stirring occasionally. Pour into a bowl and place in the refrigerator for 15 minutes until it has the consistency of buttercream.

Smooth a layer of the chocolate topping across each éclair and then chill in the refrigerator for 30 minutes until set.

Just before serving, whip the cream until it forms stiff peaks. Cut each éclair in half lengthways and use a butter knife to spread a generous quantity of the cream inside, or use a food bag to pipe it in.

Perfect for those times when you want a treat without too much preparation, this rocky road uses wholemeal savoury crackers alongside fruit and nuts to create a tempting combination of crunch and chew. Finding wholemeal crackers with no added sugar can be difficult – if you struggle, consider using rough unsweetened oatcakes instead.

Rocky Road

MAKES 16 PIECES

sunflower oil, for oiling
85g (3¼oz) soft dried apricots
75g (3oz) whole almonds
75g (3oz) whole hazelnuts
50g (2oz) wholemeal savoury crackers
85g (3¼oz) seedless raisins
150g (5oz) no-added-sugar milk chocolate

Lightly oil a 20cm (8-inch) square baking tin with a little sunflower oil.

Roughly chop the dried apricots and nuts. Break the crackers into pieces about 1–2.5cm (½–1 inch) square. Place everything in a bowl and add the raisins.

Break the chocolate into small pieces. Place in a heatproof bowl set over a saucepan of barely simmering water (make sure the base of the bowl doesn't touch the water), or in the microwave on a medium setting for about 45 seconds (my preferred method), until nearly all the chocolate has melted. Give it a stir and leave to rest for a couple of minutes until it has all melted.

Pour the melted chocolate into the bowl with the nut mixture and stir everything well together.

Transfer the mixture to the baking tin and spread it evenly until the tin has been filled. Use a spatula to smooth the surface as much as possible. Chill in the refrigerator for at least an hour until set. Cut into 16 pieces with a sharp knife. You can store the rocky road in an airtight container in the refrigerator for up to a week.

If you're a fan of caramels, you'll be very happy with these chewy chocolate treats. I've specified dark chocolate because in the stevia-sweetened brand I use there are far fewer naturally occurring sugars than the milk chocolate version, but it's up to you – these are amazing either way.

Macadamia Chews

MAKES ABOUT 16

75g (3oz) whole macadamia nuts
125g (4oz) chewy dried banana slices
2 teaspoons water
75g (3oz) no-added-sugar plain dark chocolate

Line a baking sheet with silicone baking paper.

Finely chop one macadamia nut and set aside. Using a large sharp knife, finely chop the banana slices. Place them in a food processor with the remaining nuts and measurement water. Pulse the mixture until the nuts are finely chopped and the mixture is starting to clump together. Give everything a good stir.

Take a heaped teaspoonful of the mixture and roll it firmly into a ball (if the mixture seems crumbly, add a drop more water). Place the ball on a large plate. Repeat until all the mixture has been used up.

Break the chocolate into small pieces. Place in a heatproof bowl set over a saucepan of barely simmering water (make sure the base of the bowl doesn't touch the water), or in the microwave on a medium setting for about 45 seconds (my preferred method), until nearly all the chocolate has melted. Give it a stir and leave to rest for a couple of minutes until it has all melted.

Using 2 forks, roll each ball in the melted chocolate until coated all over. Allow the excess chocolate to drain through the prongs of the forks, then place the ball on the lined baking sheet.

Once all the balls have been coated, sprinkle them with the reserved chopped macadamia nut and then place the baking sheet in the refrigerator until the chocolate has set. The chews should be kept in a cool place and eaten within a week.

Variation

If you use chocolate that is dairy free, this recipe is also suitable for vegans.

This is a simple dessert that nonetheless offers a wealth of possibilities, making it perfect as a party treat or for children. I love serving everyone their fondue in a teacup, with the assorted items for dipping, impaled on cocktail sticks, around the saucer. The question is what to dip? You could go for the usual suspects like sliced banana, sliced pineapple or strawberries, but don't discount the savoury options: salted pretzels, crispy bacon and pitted black olives are all surprisingly delicious too.

Chocolate Fondue

SERVES 6

For the fondue
150g (5oz) no-added-sugar milk chocolate, broken into small pieces
375ml (13fl oz) single cream
3 teaspoons cornflour
2 tablespoons water

To serve
selection of bite-sized food morsels, such as chopped fruit, berries and savoury crackers, for dipping

Place the chocolate with the cream in a small saucepan over a low heat until the chocolate has melted, stirring occasionally.

Mix the cornflour with the measurement water in a cup until smooth. Pour the mixture into the chocolate cream and stir to ensure everything has combined.

Gradually bring the mixture to the boil, stirring continuously, until it has the consistency of custard. Pour your fondue into 6 teacups and serve immediately, surrounded by your selection of items for dipping.

Baklava is usually steeped in a sugar syrup, but for this version I've used date purée with a hint of lemon. This provides not only sweetness but also nutrients and fibre. The overall effect is gorgeously buttery and nutty, with hints of toffee flavour. This recipe assumes a filo pastry sheet size of 30 x 40cm (12 x 16 inches).

Baklava

MAKES 12

50g (2oz) pitted dried dates, chopped
250ml (8fl oz) water
2 teaspoons fresh lemon juice
150g (5oz) raw cashew nuts, finely chopped
75g (3oz) shelled raw pistachio nuts, finely chopped
¼ teaspoon ground mixed spice
5 sheets of ready-made filo pastry, about 100g (3½oz) total weight
75g (3oz) salted butter, melted

Preheat the oven to 200°C/180°C fan/400°F/Gas Mark 6. Line a 12-cup muffin tin with paper muffin cases.

Place the dates and measurement water in a blender and blend to a purée. Transfer the purée to a saucepan and bring it to the boil. Reduce the heat to medium and simmer for 15 minutes until the mixture has thickened to the consistency of yogurt, then add the lemon juice. Stir the cashews and pistachios into the date mixture with the mixed spice.

Place the stack of filo pastry sheets lengthways. Now liberally brush melted butter on to the top of each pastry sheet. I find it easiest to do it like this: fold the right-hand side of the top sheet over the left-hand side, almost as if you were turning the pages of a book. Brush melted butter on the exposed surface of the next sheet in the stack, then turn the page, as it were, to expose the next sheet and brush that one with butter too. Continue until you reach the final sheet, then turn all the 'pages' back until your sheets are unfolded. Repeat for the left-hand side of each sheet. The final step is to butter the top sheet.

Cut the stack of pastry into 12 squares 10cm (4 inches) in size. Bring the corners of one square together to form a sort of flower shape and place it in a muffin case, then repeat for the remaining squares. Pour any remaining melted butter into the date and nut mixture and give it a stir. Place about 3 teaspoonfuls in the centre of each case until all the mixture is used up.

Bake for 20–25 minutes until the pastry has turned golden. These are best served warm, glistening and crispy from the oven.

Mint and dark chocolate are one of those fail-safe combinations. The crunch comes from oatcakes – it doesn't matter if you use the 'smooth' or 'rough' kind, just as long as they have no added sugar. I've used lucuma powder (see page 186), to add sweetness and because it's packed with nutrients, but if you prefer, you could just add 4 extra dried dates instead.

Mint Chocolate Crunch

MAKES 16 SLICES

200g (7oz) unsweetened oatcakes
100g (3½oz) pitted dried dates
100g (3½oz) unsweetened smooth
   cashew nut butter
1 tablespoon raw lucuma powder
   (see page 186)
4 teaspoons cocoa powder
2 teaspoons mint extract
100g (3½oz) unsalted butter, melted
100g (3½oz) no-added-sugar plain
   dark chocolate

Place the oatcakes, dates, cashew nut butter, lucuma powder, cocoa powder and mint extract in a food processor. Pulse until you have a rough, rubbly mixture.

....

Pour in the melted butter and stir until everything is well coated. Spoon the mixture into a 20cm (8-inch) square baking tin and spread it out evenly. Press it down firmly with the back of a metal tablespoon to compact it and flatten the surface.

....

Break the chocolate into small pieces. Place in a heatproof bowl set over a saucepan of barely simmering water (make sure the base of the bowl doesn't touch the water), or in the microwave on a medium setting for about 45 seconds (my preferred method), until nearly all the chocolate has melted. Give it a stir and leave to rest for a couple of minutes until it has all melted.

....

Spread the melted chocolate evenly across the minty biscuit base with a spatula. Chill in the refrigerator for at least an hour, and then use a sharp knife to cut it into 16 pieces. Keep in the refrigerator until ready to serve. This will keep for up to 3 days.

Variations

If your chocolate is dairy free and you use a dairy-free margarine in place of the butter, this recipe would be suitable for dairy-free and vegan diets. Use gluten-free oatcakes for a gluten free version of this recipe.

These simple snacks are great by themselves, or try them dipped into cream cheese or hot chocolate! All you need is a part-baked demi-baguette – one of those bake-at-home breads sold in convenience stores – and a few bits from the store cupboard. White baguettes are fine, but if you can find a wholemeal version, so much the better.

Cinnamon Toasts

MAKES ABOUT 40

1 part-baked demi-baguette, about 150g (5oz)
2 tablespoons sunflower oil
2 teaspoons ground cinnamon
1 teaspoon stevia powder (see page 187)

Preheat the oven to 200°C/180°C fan/400°F/Gas Mark 6.

Slice the baguette into slices about 5mm (¼ inch) thick. Brush each side with a little sunflower oil and place on a baking sheet.

Stir the cinnamon and stevia powder together. Sprinkle liberally all across the baguette slices, then shake the baking sheet to get some of the cinnamon mixture on the underside of the slices as well.

Bake for 15 minutes until the baguette slices have become completely hard. Leave them to cool on a wire rack. Store them in an airtight tin and eat within a week.

Watching a film just isn't the same without a bowl of popcorn, so if you'd like an alternative to your usual sweet flavour, try this version. The toffee taste of lucuma powder mixed with butter makes for a moreish treat.

Toffee-flavoured Popcorn

SERVES 3–4

1 tablespoon sunflower oil
85g (3¼oz) popping corn
50g (2oz) salted butter
4 tablespoons raw lucuma powder
(see page 186)
2 teaspoons stevia powder
(see page 187)

Place the oil and popcorn in an 18cm (7-inch) diameter saucepan and put the lid on. Heat over a medium heat. After about 10 minutes you'll hear the corn kernels start to pop; after about 15 minutes they should all be done. Transfer the corn to a large bowl, discarding any unpopped kernels.

Melt the butter in the saucepan that held the corn, then stir in the lucuma powder and stevia powder until combined. Pour the buttery mixture over the corn and toss the corn to get an even coating, then serve.

This is one of those very simple yet stunningly effective recipes. I love how the juicy sweet and fragrant lychees get a hit from the very finely chopped chilli, while the cream cheese prevents the combination becoming too fiery. Because chillies vary in their spiciness, choose your quantity according to how much fire you want in your final dish.

Sweet Chilli Bites

MAKES ABOUT 15

2–3 red chillies
150g (5oz) cream cheese
175g (6oz) pitted fresh or drained
    canned lychees
1 teaspoon paprika

Start by preparing the chillies. Cut the chillies in half lengthways and remove the pith and seeds, then chop the flesh extremely finely. Stir it into the cream cheese.

Use the handle of a teaspoon to fill each lychee with the cream cheese mixture. Sprinkle the finished bites with the paprika and serve.

I absolutely adore plantains, especially when they are fried in butter – add a cool smoked chilli dip and you have a great party snack. Make sure your plantains have turned black before you use them, though, and don't forget the cocktail sticks!

Butter-fried Plantains with Smoky Dip

SERVES 4

4 tablespoons crème fraîche
grated rind of 1 unwaxed lime and
   ½ teaspoon juice
½ teaspoon chipotle paste
3 ripe plantains, about 550g
   (1lb 2oz) total weight
25g (1oz) salted butter

To make the dip, place the crème fraîche in a serving bowl, then stir in the lime rind and juice and the chipotle paste (use only ¼ teaspoon of the paste if you prefer just a hint of heat).

Top and tail the plantains, then lightly run a knife down each one to split the skin. Remove the skin and slice the plantains on a slant into pieces roughly 1cm (½ inch) thick.

Heat the butter in a frying pan and fry the plantains over a medium-high heat for about 1–2 minutes per side until browned. Serve them as soon as they are done, with the dip alongside.

Sauces, Spreads & Other Basics

The natural sweetness of rice milk is combined with spices to create this ultra-smooth, rich chocolate drink. The topping of whipped cream and chopped pistachios makes it utterly indulgent.

Velvet Hot Chocolate

SERVES 2

175ml (6fl oz) whipping cream
1 teaspoon cornflour
750ml (1¼ pints) rice milk
2 green cardamom pods
½ teaspoon ground cinnamon, plus extra for serving
6 teaspoons cocoa powder
1 teaspoon chopped unsalted pistachio nuts

Whip the cream until it forms firm peaks and set aside.

Mix the cornflour with a couple of tablespoons of the rice milk in a cup until smooth. Break the cardamom pods open and remove the seeds. Crush them with the back of a teaspoon.

Place the crushed cardamom seeds in a saucepan with the cinnamon and cocoa over a medium heat. Add the remaining rice milk and stir in the cornflour mixture. Continue stirring until the mixture boils and thickens to a consistency similar to cows' milk. Divide between 2 tall heatproof glasses or mugs.

Spoon or pipe the whipped cream on top of the hot chocolate and sprinkle with the chopped pistachios and a dusting of cinnamon. Serve immediately.

Variation

Served without the cream, this hot chocolate is also suitable for vegan/dairy-free diets.

Thanks to the ground almonds, this buttery, crisp dessert pastry has fewer carbohydrates than regular pastry, plus more nutrients and fibre. It is also very quick to make!

Low-carb Dessert Pastry

MAKES ABOUT 275G (9OZ)

100g (3½oz) plain flour
50g (2oz) ground almonds
75g (3oz) unsalted butter, chilled
  and cut into chunks
1 egg, beaten

Place the flour, ground almonds and butter in a food processor. Pulse until you have a mixture with the texture of coffee grounds.

Pour the egg into the flour mixture and then pulse until all the ingredients come together as a yellow dough. Remove the dough from the food processor. It is now ready for use as directed in your recipe.

If you want to make a pastry case only (blind baking), preheat the oven to 200°C/180°C fan/400°F/Gas Mark 6. Roll out the pastry on a worktop well dusted with flour to a thickness of about 3–4mm (about ⅛ inch) and then cut it a little larger than the intended tin. Press the pastry into the tin and trim the excess with a sharp knife. Add a layer of foil, then pour in dried beans or baking beans to fill the pastry case. Bake for 20 minutes until crisp and just turning golden brown.

Dried milk makes a winning substitute for icing sugar when it comes to frosting. I've formulated 4 common flavours that should give options for every occasion.

Whipped Cake Frosting

MAKES ENOUGH FOR 12 CUPCAKES OR 1 LARGE CAKE

For the basic frosting
250g (8oz) unsalted butter,
  very soft, cut into chunks
100g (3½oz) dried milk powder
4 teaspoons stevia powder
  (see page 187)
pinch of salt
2 teaspoons water

For vanilla frosting
2 teaspoons unsweetened vanilla
  extract

For chocolate frosting
25g (1oz) cocoa powder
2 tablespoons raw lucuma powder
  (see page 186)

For coffee frosting
1 tablespoon raw lucuma powder
  (see page 186)
1 teaspoon unsweetened vanilla
  extract
2 teaspoons instant coffee granules
1 tablespoon boiling water

For zesty frosting
3 tablespoons fresh lemon juice
3 teaspoons grated lime rind

Place the butter in a large bowl. Sift in the milk powder, crushing any larger granules with the back of a teaspoon until it has all passed through the sieve. Whisk everything together thoroughly using an electric whisk. Stir the stevia powder and salt into the measurement water in a cup until dissolved. Whisk into the butter mixture until you have a pale mixture with a light texture. The frosting is now ready to be flavoured from the choices below.

For vanilla frosting, whisk the frosting and vanilla extract together until thoroughly combined. The frosting is now ready to use.

For chocolate frosting, sift the cocoa and lucuma powder into the frosting and whisk together to create a smooth, rich paste ready to ice your cake.

For coffee frosting, add the lucuma powder and vanilla extract to the frosting. Dissolve the coffee granules in the measurement boiling water and pour into the frosting. Whisk everything together until thoroughly combined. The frosting is now ready to use.

For zesty frosting, whisk the lemon juice into the frosting, then stir in the lime rind. The frosting is now ready to use.

Note
Keep frosted cakes in the refrigerator until needed and eat the frosting within 48 hours.

Use this silky white sauce cold as a low-fat alternative to cream, or hot instead of regular vanilla custard. Rice milk gives a wonderful natural sweetness, while the vanilla pod adds a touch of luxury.

Vanilla Cream

MAKES ABOUT 500ML (17FL OZ)

325ml (11fl oz) rice milk
1 vanilla pod
2 tablespoons cornflour
½ teaspoon stevia powder (see page 187)
175ml (6fl oz) single cream

Pour the rice milk into a small saucepan. Carefully cut down the length of the vanilla pod and scrape out the seeds into the rice milk, then add the empty pod as well. Bring to the boil, then remove the pod.

Mix the cornflour and stevia powder with the cream in a bowl until smooth. Whisk into the hot rice milk and bring to the boil, whisking continously. The mixture will thicken to the consistency of Greek yogurt.

Remove from the heat and pour it into a jug. You can either serve it immediately, or leave it to cool completely before giving it another quick stir and serving it cold.

This buttery orange sauce is just perfect for pancakes – or if you are feeling really indulgent, you could use it on my Vanilla Ice Cream (see page 89) in place of syrupy toppings. If you want to maximize your nutrients, use 4 large, freshly squeezed oranges instead of juice from a carton.

Orange Dessert Sauce

MAKES ABOUT 300ML (½ PINT)

500ml (17fl oz) fresh orange juice with bits
100g (3½oz) unsalted butter, chopped
1 teaspoon cornflour
½ teaspoon stevia powder (see page 187)

Set 2 tablespoons of the orange juice aside, then heat the rest in a saucepan until it boils. Add the butter and stir until it has melted. Leave the mixture to boil for 10 minutes until it has reduced by about one-third.

Mix the cornflour and stevia powder into the reserved orange juice in a bowl until smooth. Whisk into the hot boiling butter/juice mixture and bring to the boil, whisking continuously. The mixture will thicken to the consistency of thick cream.

Remove the sauce from the heat and use immediately.

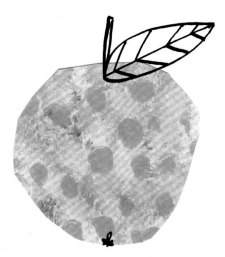

Coulis is a fancy name for a dessert sauce and most standard recipes contain added sugar. This mango version uses just fresh fruit and takes only moments to make. Try it poured over my Fresh Fig Panna Cotta (see page 82), drizzled over a cream cake or even served alongside roast chicken.

Mango Coulis

MAKES ABOUT 150ML (¼ PINT)

1 medium ripe mango (about 300g/10oz), peeled and stone removed

2 tablespoons fresh orange juice with bits, plus extra if needed

Place the mango flesh and orange juice in a blender and blend until smooth.

Rub the mixture through a sieve to leave a smooth purée with the consistency of yogurt. It should be quite easy to pour. If the coulis seems too thick, add a drop more orange juice. This is best used the same day.

A compote of mixed berries is an easy way to boost your fruit intake: try it on porridge, with pancakes or simply topped with a little natural yogurt. This recipe works well with fresh or frozen berries.

Mixed Berry Compote

SERVES 3–4

200g (7oz) fresh or frozen mixed raspberries, blackberries and blackcurrants
1 banana, about 150g (5oz)

Place the berries in a saucepan. Peel and mash the banana, then add to the pan over a medium-low heat. Place the lid on the pan and cook for 10–15 minutes, stirring occasionally. The compote is done when the banana seems to have disappeared and you are left with a juicy mixture but with most of the berries still reasonably intact.

You can serve the compote warm or cold. It will keep for up to 3 days in the refrigerator.

Variation

You can use other types of berries for this compote, as long as there are always some naturally sweeter ones like strawberries, raspberries or blueberries alongside the more sour varieties such as blackcurrants or gooseberries.

This tangy orange and apricot curd is perfect for spreading on crumpets, toast or scones, and also makes a delicious filling and/or topping for a cake.

Orange & Apricot Curd

MAKES ABOUT 250ML (8FL OZ)

100g (3½oz) dried apricots
125ml (4fl oz) water
grated rind of 1 small unwaxed
   orange and 3 tablespoons juice
1 egg
50g (2oz) unsalted butter, chopped
pinch of salt

Soak the apricots in the measurement water for 4 hours or overnight.

Place the apricots in a blender, add the orange rind and juice and egg. Blend the mixture until smooth.

Transfer the apricot mixture to a small saucepan with the butter and salt. Heat gently until the butter melts, stirring continuously. Continue cooking for about 5–10 minutes until the mixture has become so thick that you can't see the base of the pan as you stir.

Remove the pan from the heat and leave the curd to cool completely before transferring it to an airtight jar. It will keep for up to a week in the refrigerator.

Jams were originally invented as a way to preserve fruit out of season – and just also happened to be delicious on toast. However, what with modern refrigeration and year-round fresh fruit, drowning strawberries in sugar is not essential any more. But if you still want something for toast, here's how.

Strawberry Jam

MAKES ABOUT 250ML (8FL OZ)

1 dessert apple, about 175g (6oz), cored and roughly grated (leave the skin on)

200g (7oz) fresh strawberries, hulled and roughly chopped

2 teaspoons stevia powder (see page 187)

½ teaspoon fresh lemon juice

Place all the ingredients in a saucepan with a tight-fitting lid and cook over a medium heat for 20 minutes, stirring occasionally. At the end of this time, the apple will have lost most of its structure and the strawberries will have spread their red juices throughout the mix.

Take the lid off the pan, turn the heat up a notch and let the jam bubble gently for 5 minutes or so until it thickens. Leave to cool.

You can either store the jam in airtight jar in the refrigerator for up to a week or, if you prefer handy portions that will last longer than this, divide the jam between the sections of an ice cube tray, then cover with foil and freeze. That way, you can defrost it as and when necessary.

Standard chocolate hazelnut spreads are loaded with sugar, but making your own is surprisingly quick and easy to do. This recipe provides a reasonably small amount, but it's best to make it little and often because there is no sugar to act as a preservative.

Chocolate Hazelnut Spread

MAKES ABOUT 125ML (4FL OZ)

20g (¾oz) raw hazelnuts, roughly chopped
4 tablespoons sunflower oil
25g (1oz) dried milk powder
1 tablespoon cocoa powder
2 teaspoons stevia powder (see page 187)
4 tablespoons boiling water

Toast the chopped hazelnuts in a dry frying pan over a medium-high heat for 3–4 minutes, stirring occasionally, until they have turned golden brown.

Place the nuts with the oil, milk powder and cocoa powder in jug. Use a stick blender to blend everything together until you have a dark, oily and somewhat grainy mixture. This will take up to a minute.

Stir the stevia powder into the measurement boiling water in a cup until dissolved. While continuing to blend, slowly pour the stevia mixture into the nut mixture. Suddenly everything will combine into a smooth paste. Transfer it to a small airtight jar and refrigerate. Once it has chilled it will have the consistency of soft butter.

The spread will keep in the refrigerator for up to 3 days. It also freezes well – just allow it to defrost and give it a stir before use.

Chutneys and pickles are relatively sugary foods, so if you want to cut back on sugar, it makes sense to reduce the amount you consume in this way. My quick pickle won't keep for longer than a few days and is sweetened only with apple, but it still makes a tasty accompaniment to cold meats and cheeses.

Quick Apple Pickle

MAKES ABOUT 200ML (7FL OZ)

1 teaspoon sunflower oil
1 small dessert apple, peeled, cored
   and finely chopped
½ small onion, finely chopped
4 tablespoons apple purée
1 tablespoon sultanas
1 teaspoon cider vinegar
1 teaspoon wholegrain mustard
½ teaspoon ground ginger
½ teaspoon ground coriander
pinch of salt

Heat the oil in a saucepan and fry the apple and onion over a medium-high heat for 3–4 minutes until the apple has softened and the onion has become slightly translucent.

Remove from the heat and stir in all the remaining ingredients. Leave to cool, then store in an airtight jar in the refrigerator for up to 3 days.

This homemade sauce makes a good alternative to ready-made sweet chilli sauces, which often have added sugar. It has a piquant sweet-and-sour flavour that is great as an accompaniment to spring rolls, dumplings or sushi.

Asian-style Dipping Sauce

MAKES ABOUT 75ML (3FL OZ)

4 tablespoons good-quality fresh apple juice
1 tablespoon light soy sauce
½ teaspoon garlic purée
¼ teaspoon ground ginger
1 teaspoon rice wine vinegar or cider vinegar
¼ hot red chilli, deseeded and thinly sliced
1 teaspoon finely chopped chives

Stir the apple juice and soy sauce together in a small serving bowl. Mix the garlic purée and ginger into the vinegar in a cup until smooth, then stir into the apple juice/soy mixture.

Add the chilli and chives, then serve.

Variation

Make this sauce gluten free by using gluten-free tamari in place of the soy sauce.

Ketchup is around 25 per cent sugar – it's practically jam!
– which is why, of course, it tastes so good. The sugar and
vinegar are designed to preserve it, but it's easy to make
a quick version in small batches and keep it in the refrigerator.
There is still sweetness here, but it comes only from the fruits
and is accompanied by their nutrients as well.

Tomato Ketchup

MAKES ABOUT 50ML (2FL OZ)

2 tablespoons apple purée
1 tablespoon tomato purée
1 teaspoon cider vinegar
½ teaspoon garlic purée
pinch of ground black pepper
pinch of ground allspice

Place all the ingredients in a bowl and stir well. The ketchup is now ready
to serve, but if you don't want to use it all at once, transfer to an airtight
container and place in the refrigerator – it will keep for up to a week.

There are many, many uses for this creamy egg-free mayo – it's great in a chicken sandwich, super-tasty smothered on new potatoes and perfect as a dip. I love it because it's easy to make and full of avocado goodness, without any added sweeteners.

Avocado Mayonnaise

MAKES ABOUT 150ML (¼ PINT)

150g (5oz) avocado flesh (about 1 avocado)
85ml (3¼fl oz) olive oil
1 tablespoon cornflour
2 tablespoons fresh lemon juice
1½ teaspoons garlic purée

Place all the ingredients in a blender and blend until thick and completely smooth – about 2 minutes or so. Leave to sit for a couple of minutes. Now blend again for a further minute. This method helps the mayonnaise to stay creamy and prevent it from separating.

Serve immediately or scrape everything into an airtight container and refrigerate until needed. Give it a quick stir before serving. It will keep for up to 3 days without going brown.

Many prepared salad dressings contain hidden sugar, so making your own is a good way to eliminate unnecessary carbs from your diet. This recipe will give you a good basic vinaigrette. You can then play around with the formula by using different kinds of oil or vinegar, or by adding other flavourings such as chopped herbs or mustard powder.

Vinaigrette Dressing

MAKES ABOUT 75ML (3FL OZ)

4 tablespoons olive oil
1 tablespoon white wine vinegar
1 teaspoon garlic purée
large pinch of ground black pepper

Place all the ingredients in a pot with a lid, then shake thoroughly before drizzling over your salad. The dressing will keep for a couple of weeks in the refrigerator.

Variation

You can make a creamy dressing by adding 2 tablespoons crumbled feta cheese or blue cheese and 1 tablespoon single cream to the dressing and whisking everything together thoroughly before use. The dressing will keep for a couple of days in the refrigerator.

Glossary

The following is a guide to some of the sweeteners and more unusual ingredients that I use in my recipes.

Agar powder

Agar (or agar agar) powder is a natural gelling agent that comes from freeze-dried seaweed. Suitable for vegetarians and vegans, it helps to prevent the growth of ice crystals in frozen foods and give a satiny mouthfeel to ice cream. It is sometimes sold as flakes. If you can't find agar powder, carrageenan powder (made from another kind of seaweed) can be used instead.

Almond milk

This dairy-free alternative to cows' milk is made from a filtered blend of almonds and water, and provides an assortment of nutrients. Make sure the product you choose is unsweetened; it is naturally sugar free. You can use soya milk instead if you prefer.

Apple purée

I use apple purée to sweeten some of my dishes. It can be tricky to find, but the baby food aisle of the supermarket is a good place to source it, especially if only a small amount is needed. If you want to make your own, finely chop a peeled, cored cooking apple and heat gently in a saucepan with 2 tablespoons apple juice until the apple has become pulpy. Leave to cool before use.

Chestnut flour

Made from ground dried chestnuts, chestnut flour is naturally gluten free. High in fibre and very nutritious, it also has a natural sugar content of about 20 per cent, which means that chestnut flour can be used as a wheat flour substitute in cakes with few, if any, further sweeteners needed.

Evaporated milk

This is milk that has been boiled for a long time until it becomes thick and gloopy, a process that concentrates its natural sugar (lactose) content. It can be useful in some recipes, though it has a distinctive taste. It usually comes in a can. Evaporated milk is not to be confused with condensed milk, which has added sugar.

Honey

Chemically speaking, honey is not much different to diluted table sugar, though good quality honey also contains a mixture of minerals and other nutrients. I use it very sparingly and always choose a raw local organic honey.

No-added-sugar chocolate

As distinct from unsweetened chocolate (which is rather bitter), no-added-sugar chocolate is still somewhat sweet but is sweetened without sugar. It is sometimes marketed as diabetic chocolate. The brand I use contains stevia, but look out for others sweetened with erythritol or maltitol, which are low-calorie naturally derived sweeteners. If you can't find them in your supermarket, try health food shops or online suppliers. Normally both dark and milk versions are available. This kind of chocolate is   useful for adding a touch of luxury to desserts and cake, but bear in mind that it is still high in calories.

Raw lucuma powder

This low-GI sweetener comes from a nutritious South American fruit with a very hard flesh, which is ground up into a powder that has a malty toffee–date flavour. It is useful in some recipes, but the drawback is that the powder doesn't dissolve, so it's not suitable as a sugar alternative for sprinkling on doughnuts or cereal, for instance, because it will just taste 'claggy'.

Rice milk

Made from blended rice, water and oil, rice milk should not contain any added sweeteners. Although the total sugar content is the same as cows' milk (about 4 per cent), it tastes sweeter. This is useful in recipes because it means that the need for further sweetening is reduced.

Stevia powder

I use the term 'stevia powder' in my recipes to refer to sweeteners based on stevia extracts. There are many such products on the market and the precise extract of the stevia plant used varies, as does the added ingredients. I like stevia because it is naturally derived and only a little is needed. I keep the amounts of stevia I use to a minimum – just enough to make the recipes pleasantly sweet, but without the aftertaste becoming noticeable. The brand I use has added erythritol, a low calorie, naturallly derived sweetener, and is about three times sweeter than ordinary white sugar. But don't feel you have to use stevia powder at all – there are many other alternative sweeteners available.

Index

Acknowledgements

To the STARS, may they always shine.

Author's acknowledgements
For support and practical help of many kinds I want to thank Mum and Dad, Richard, Phil, Chris and Maureen; Hannah Booth, Hannah Johnston and Jason Taylor at DFC; Allyson Bates; Zoe Bailey; Becky Boyd; Ruth Gillingham; Nina Hertig; Becky and Chris Knapp; Allison Macfarlan; Esther Porta; Lucie Roberts; Helen Rossiter and Andrea Wood.

Thank you to everyone who tested my recipes, including Anne and Matt Balme, Anna Barrett, Jacky Booth, Tania Fish, Kim and Richard Lankshear, Rose Lewis, Felicia Parker and Eric Trolle.

Thank you to my agent Eve White and her assistant Jack Ramm for their ideas. At Octopus I am grateful as ever to Stephanie, Alex, Jaz, Abigail and the rest of the team for such a beautiful book. Thanks too to Kat Mead, Siân Henley, and Liz and Max Haarala Hamilton, who helped to bring the recipes to life and gave me some brilliant memories, especially when it comes to citrus.

About the author
Susanna Booth is a passionate and inventive self-taught chef who specializes in creating recipes for specific dietary requirements. A former recipe columnist for the Guardian, she uses her degree in Polymer Chemistry to offer a fresh perspective on some of our best-loved dishes.

An Hachette UK Company
www.hachette.co.uk
First published in Great Britain in 2016
by Hamlyn, a division of
Octopus Publishing Group Ltd
Carmelite House
50 Victoria Embankment
London EC4Y 0DZ
www.octopusbooks.co.uk

First published as *Sensationally Sugar Free* in 2016
This paperback edition published in 2017

ISBN 978 0 60063 485 0

A CIP catalogue record for this book is available from the British Library

Printed and bound in China

10 9 8 7 6 5 4 3 2 1

Publishing Director - Stephanie Jackson
Art Director - Jonathan Christie
Design - Jaz Bahra
Senior Editor - Alex Stetter
Copy Editor – Jo Richardson
Ilustrations - Abigail Read
Photography - Haarala Hamilton
Home Economist and Food Stylist - Kat Mead
Nutritionist - Angela Dowden
Production Controller - Meskerem Berhane